NEW CREATI

Catharina J. M. Halkes

New Creation

CHRISTIAN FEMINISM AND THE RENEWAL
OF THE EARTH

First published in Holland as ... *En Alles Zal Worden Herschapen*
in 1989 by Uitgeverij Ten Have bv
Prinses Marielaan 8
Postbus 1
3740 AA Baarn

First published in Great Britain 1991
SPCK
Holy Trinity Church
Marylebone Road
London NW1 4DU

British Library Cataloguing in Publication Data
Halkes, Catharina J. M.
New creation.
I. Title
II. [En alles zal worden herschapen. *English*]
262.15

ISBN 0–282–04539–9

Typeset by J&L Composition Ltd,
Filey, North Yorkshire
Printed in Great Britain by
Biddles Ltd, Guildford and Kings Lynn

To Mary Grey,
my successor in the chair of 'Feminism and Christianity' at the
Catholic University of Nijmegen, who has become a dear and
inspiring friend,
and to Ruth and Loren Halvorson
of the ARC Retreat Community, Minnesota, for whose
friendship and help during their sabbatical stay in Nijmegen I
am deeply grateful.

CONTENTS

Introduction   1

Part One

1   Woman Between Nature and Culture   10
2   'Mother' Nature   19
3   *Man*-aging Nature   33
4   Women, Slaves, and Savages   41
5   Knowing Nature   50
6   Woman's 'Nature'   63

Part Two

7   God's Good Creation   74
8   A New Relation Between Nature and Culture   92
9   Ecology and Feminism   108
10 Women and Men – Image of God   128
11 '. . . And All Shall Be Recreated'   151

    Bibliography   163
    Index of Names   175

INTRODUCTION

1

The immediate inducement for writing this book is the World Council of Churches' appeal for a world-wide conciliar process to reconsider the meaning of justice, peace, and the becoming-whole of creation. These heavy-laden terms offer hints of a perspective rather than indicating the already obvious.

It is an excellent initiative and has elicited exciting responses (at any rate here in the Netherlands). Many books and thematic issues of periodicals have been produced on these subjects. Numerous conferences have also been devoted to the issues.

In this study I want to take a closer look at this complex question. I am convinced that there is not only a clear connection between these three important themes, but that they also share a common basis. In my opinion, a complicated issue lies hidden here. Our present political and ecological crisis, caused by the absence of justice, peace and particularly of reverence and respect for creation, is in my view also caused by the disastrous one-sidedness of our culture. Our Western society is coloured and characterized by a predominantly masculine outlook on life, exemplified by a technology and policy which accepts interruption and criticism only with difficulty. Yet this criticism is becoming increasingly louder as concern for the way matters are developing grows.

An important voice in this chorus of protest and concern comes from women who have become aware of their own position and of the structures in society and in the Churches. They reflect upon their existence and faith and discover ever more clearly the structure of masculine dominance. This is as true for our culture's values and norms as it is for practical political policy.

Under this visible surface is another factor, namely, images, the concepts our culture has of both 'nature' and 'woman'. There is a tendency to view nature and women in the same perspective, while men consider themselves creators of culture.

This is a complicated problem which is not easy to explain, let alone solve. Yet I think it is necessary to examine it in order to work our way to at least one of its roots. One-sidedness is, by definition, an imbalance providing only a partial view of society and culture.

This is the reason to write this book. It must be possible to dredge up from the deeper layers of our consciousness the putative connection between woman and nature, man and culture, and also to explain it.

The time has come to develop a greater respect for nature, not only to assure our survival, but primarily because nature has its own dignity, a characteristic we seem to have forgotten.

That women also have their own dignity and character is at present admitted, at least verbally. This admission, however, is often formal and superficial, and is only shallowly rooted in human awareness. Men are not alone in missing this awareness. There are also many women who have so internalized the existing projections of themselves that their actions appear to be natural.

This book is expressly intended for women *and* men, for all who are involved in the conciliar process. It aims to help our contemplation of the more deep-seated causes of the inequality of power between women and men and the division between nature and culture. Only in this way can we approach the causes instead of only trying to cure the symptoms.

The most gratifying result for which I could hope would be that this study would become the theme of a continuous dialogue which leads to deeper mutual understanding.

As my study progressed, what the complexities of the theme are became ever clearer. That is why the book has become unavoidably complicated. I am well aware that what is presented here is only a beginning and that much specialized investigation is needed before a clear and accessible study becomes available.

I advise those who find Part 1 unmanageable not to struggle through all the chapters (I am thinking particularly of Chapter 5), but to go directly to Part 2. Each chapter can be read as a separate unit, since each treats a separate aspect of the whole. Of course each chapter relates to the whole, but each has its own specific focus.

To preview the book's major contours, I would like to sketch here its structure. Fundamentally, there are three themes running through the book: nature, woman, and image-formation. The whole is put in the context of the World Council's conciliar process.

Part 1 highlights the various images of nature and woman from diverse points of view. Part 2 is more theologically orientated and treats nature as creation, 'woman and man as images of God', and argues for a renewed ecological theology.

Chapter One

I begin with the general question as it is studied in cultural anthropology. Among all the differences apparent in the distinctive cultures, there is still nearly always a certain inequality in power to be noted between men and women. The question is then: To what degree does this difference in esteem have to do with the association of women with nature?

Chapter Two

The oldest image of nature has always been Woman or Mother. As such, she was revered as long as nature, and especially the earth, was viewed as an organism inspiring awe. As soon as technology was developed, awe was replaced by an aggressive will to dominate.

Chapter Three

Rationalism, a philosophy which not only objectifies nature, but which reduces everything but the thinking subject itself to lifeless material, to things, goes one step further. This, too, leads to a decreased repect of nature. It also causes a deep separation between spirit (*ratio*) and body. Now, since women are predominantly associated with their corporeality and with nature, this is not a positive development.

Chapter Four

To have a clearer view of this, I turn to Aristotle, one of the most important philosophers of classical antiquity. In his political philosophy he distinguishes between 'body people' and spiritual or 'head people'. To deal with this Aristotelian view in our feminist awakening we have come to realize that not only are women subject to marginalization and objectification, but so too are all 'others', e.g. 'lower' classes, non-white races. They share the fate of being dominated along with nature. This hierarchical and instrumental thinking keeps the dominant male class in place. In an excursus on hunting we also hear many aggressive terms expressing conquest and war and an ambivalent relationship to nature.

Chapter Five

Next I look to the field of epistemology and the relationship between the researcher and the object investigated – nature – as well as to the metaphors used for this relationship. It is noteworthy that 'love metaphors' are still used and that 'knowledge' can mean here erotic or sexual 'knowledge'. There are only a few examples: Plato uses 'knowledge' to mean pairing, following a homo-erotic model which is regressive and non-aggressive; but basically he uses it in a thought pattern which separates the sensual world from that of the ideas; Bacon uses a patriarchal model of marriage; scientists still using organic models use the image of coitus. These different models each express relationships based either on power or on equality recurring between the male and the female.

Chapter Six

The next step is an investigation of the diverse meanings given to 'nature' in the period between the seventeenth and the nineteenth centuries, and of the images the same philosophers and writers attribute to women's existence and their 'essence' (their 'nature'). Here too the examples given are limited but extremely clear.

The *leitmotif* of Part 1 is man's (the male's) relationship to nature. This latter is seen first as organism and later as a machine, but in both cases as female or even as 'thing'. The dominant, Western, white, and patriarchal culture's relationship to women and to all those marginalized becomes visible at the same time. The split thinking, the dualism of subject and object, is continually observable in this relationship. In this presentation I have not kept strictly to chronological order. Plato and Aristotle do not come first, but are discussed only later, where the development of their ideas is illustrative of my theme.

Part 1 is to be understood as a prelude, an introduction aiming

to clarify a number of points, in order to illuminate the theme of
Part 2, which occupies us all, namely, How do we reach a
relationship of justice, of peace and especially of respect for
the inviolability of creation? I hope that clarification of the
male–female relationship can help us find an answer.

Chapter Seven

Part 2 opens with a chapter on a theology of creation which has
yet to be developed in order to arrive at the ecological theology
that is so urgently needed. This is necessary since creation has
had too little attention as a separate category in the various
religious traditions where all the stress has been put on the
covenant. But creation has its own irreplaceable meaning. The
God of creation is also a God of blessings who remains bound to
'his' creation. The Sabbath is also discussed: a time of letting go,
rest, praise and contemplation.

But before all of this I look at the varying interpretations of
Genesis 1.26–8: 'subdue the earth' or 'dominate the earth'. These
words have caused much misunderstanding and have seduced
people into dominating nature, creation, instead of preserving
and protecting it.

Chapter Eight

Honesty requires it to be said that even before the theological
renewal, the ecological movement already existed and was already
sending out alarm signals. Here again the area of tension between
natue and culture arises. This time in the context of ecological
thinking. I then discuss the relationship of the natural sciences
and of technology to our environment. And finally I return once
more to the relationship of the searcher to his/her object, nature,
in order to point out that in the mean time a more empathetic,
heartfelt, loving relationship has come into existence – one aiming
not at dominating, but at 'interacting'.

Chapter Nine

The feminist movement also had its start in the Sixties, alongside
the new ecological movement. From its very start it was
interested in nature and ecology. Some even speak of 'eco-
feminism' and of a feminist ecological theology. Common perspectives and desires are discussed in this chapter, along with a

number of aspects of a new spirituality evolving within this movement.

Chapter Ten

Next I treat the difficulties of a modern, more adequate theological anthropology involving a reflection on the vocation, mission and goal of humanity as man and woman, in the light of creation, redemption and resurrection. It appears both risky and irrelevant to speak of woman's (or man's) unique 'nature'. Together and individually each have received the same task to fulfil, and are created according to God's image and likeness. At this point I also give my critical review of Cardinal Simonis'[1] article on feminist theology. I conclude this chapter with a few thoughts on the meaning of human sexuality; on men's particular problems in their relationships with women, and with their own bodies; on violence in our culture, and on pornography.

Chapter Eleven

After treating so much difficult material, I take the liberty in the final chapter of dreaming a utopian fantasy, of seeking new and more relevant images, both of God's creation and of humanity (as man and woman). I hope that the previous ten chapters will have provided an impetus towards the dismantling of misleading and dangerous images of 'woman and 'nature'. New images are needed, for the present and the future, not to force but to inspire.

2

I am aware that this book is a risky enterprise. It is a literary study and report of my search, and nothing more. I have dared to enter diverse fields and consult various disciplines in which I am not expert. This exploration was necessary to have a grasp of the interrelationship of the different problems.

I expect that specialists will correct numerous details. I hope, above all, that the time will come when a number of specialists, each in a different area, will undertake new studies in which the same problem will be more scientifically and precisely considered.

[1] The Cardinal-Archbishop of Utrecht, the Netherlands.

This is not a feminist book in the usual sense. I have consulted many new scientific publications written by men, in addition to the more critical feminist literature. I have consciously chosen to do this in order to enter into discussion with the many men working in the conciliar process whose familiar terrain I also wish to enter here.

This publication is also outside the category of 'women's studies'. It is simultaneously less and perhaps more. It is less, in that I have not studied one single phenomenon or aspect, either historically or systematically, which would advance scientific investigation in the area of women's studies. This book's plan is far more humble. It is more, in that, by following larger trends and taking a more global approach, it tries to show how the different phenomena are connected. It aims to be a modest contribution to the laying bare of the foundations of Western culture and towards indicating the changes necessary – necessary not only for survival, but to live humanly and creatively and to leave our children prospects for the future.

This book is therefore an invitation to men and women to work hand in hand on the basis of newly won insights. As a theologian, I consider this an important task at the present time, particularly since the World Council of Churches has initiated a decade of church solidarity with women.

There are three authors to whose work I am very much indebted: Carolyn Merchant, Evelyn Fox Keller and Gerard Liedke.

One note to avoid misunderstanding: in this study I have repeatedly used the terms 'men' and 'male'. I do not intend in doing so to generalize universally and without nuance. These terms reflect above all the dominant ruling culture and the attitudes derived from it.

Although I believe that 'God' can be thought of as both male and female, I have maintained in the theological chapters the 'customary' way of describing God as 'male', certainly when I quote an author. In the last chapter I discontinued this and alternately dreamed of God as 'he' and 'she'.

The biblical passages for the English version are cited from *The Common Bible: Revised Standard Version, an Ecumenical Edition* (London: Collins, 1973). The Bibliography contains the books and articles I have consulted. Although not all of them have been cited directly in my book, they have all certainly influenced my thinking.

Finally, a word about the title of this book. When I was a child we always prayed the prayer of the Holy Spirit at home. From the very beginning I was inspired and intrigued by the words 'Send forth Your Spirit and all shall be recreated; and You will renew the face of the earth'. Not only through our activity, but also through our receptivity to the Spirit's work will we be able to co-operate in a 'new creation'.

3

Of course I also wish to thank here those who have helped me during the last year in one way or another to produce this study. I think first of all of my three children who loyally sympathized with their writing mother who, alas, had so little time for them. The same holds true for my sister, whose sympathy continued to grow although we could see one another less often.

There have also been interested people who never ceased giving me tips about new or relevant literature. Such kindness enriched my knowledge and warmed my spirit. Therefore a word of thanks is in order for the theologian Geertrui Westeroven van Meeteren and for Gerrit Huizer, director of the Third World Center. I gladly expand this word of thanks to friends such as Dirkje Donders and Diel Stockmann van der Kallen. I am very grateful to Wil Kamminga for her help in preparing the Bibliography.

I am also happy that my youngest son, Caspar and Annelies van Heyst were kind enough to read my text and offer their critical and fruitful commentary. To them I give my heartfelt thanks.

A conversation with Piet Bennema, who is a professor of solid state chemistry and crystal formation, has made me more aware of the traps and tight corners hidden in 'holistic thinking'. Although I have been unable to include his comments completely in my text, I am grateful him for this constructive discussion and for the literature relevant to it.

My greatest thanks go to Frans Haarsma, who not only provided an extensive and professional commentary on each chapter, suggesting various changes, but – more importantly – who sympathized intensely as a true friend in this strenuous period and gave me courage when I ran the risk of losing it. Without his continuous support I could not have done it.

Finally, I would like to express my appreciation for my original Dutch publisher, Ton van der Worp. He needed patience when I had not yet finished by the date I myself had suggested. He continued to show calm and lasting trust in the meaning and success of this undertaking.

1

WOMAN BETWEEN NATURE AND CULTURE

Women are often associated with nature and men with culture. This has led to a lively discussion among cultural anthropologists. Sherry Ortner has played an important role in this, and section 1 is therefore devoted to her work. In section 2 I look at several authors who react critically to Ortner's position.

1

Ortner, a well-known cultural anthropologist, published an article in the 1970s, 'Is Female to Male as Nature is to Culture? This pithy title alone set me thinking at the time. The article drew much attention and led to a fruitful debate among her colleagues, some of whose reactions were collected in *Nature, Culture and Gender*, edited by Carol MacCormack and Marilyn Strathern.

Ortner starts from a phenomenon observed in nearly all cultures where people live and work, namely, that women have a second-class position. At the same time she notes that this phenomenon by no means takes a single form but that the precise situation of women differs from culture to culture.

Just these differences should make us careful and hesitant about attributing too rapidly a universality to the various forms of women's subservience. Ortner lists three types of data which can lead to responsible observations on this point when closely examining separate societies. They are:
– external explicit data which show that a cultural ideology considers women's tasks and roles less important and gives them less prestige;
– implicit characteristics such as attributing to women impurity and defilement because of their bodily processes, indicating a lower evaluation;

– visible evidence in the social culture that women are excluded from participation in and involvement with spheres of power in public life (Ortner 1974, pp. 69–70).

These three phenomena can take different forms in each culture, but they nearly alway recur, regardless of how they may be expressed.

We are intrigued by the question why this happens. In academic anthropology there is a general agreement that biological determinism is not involved. The different physical structures and sexual appendages do not in themselves point to a 'natural' superiority of the man or a 'natural' inferiority of the woman. That is not the problem. We have instead to look at the range of values adhered to, and the meanings given to behaviour, thus at what we call culture. Then we come back to Ortner's formulation of the question: Does the woman (or feminine) relate to the man (or masculine) as nature to culture?

The question then arises, What *is* culture? Lewis and Short's Latin dictionary gives the following meanings to the verb *colere*, from which 'culture' and 'cult' are derived: (1) an agricultural term, to cultivate, to manipulate; (2) in general, to inhabit, to occupy; (3) transitively, to care for, to decorate, to exercise (an art or science); (4) to revere, to worship (the gods); to honour, to respect, to pay homage to.

This is an interesting series of meanings, from ploughing the earth, to building and inhabiting a house, to giving form to consciousness and creating beautiful things.

This means that as soon as a given element is adapted and provided with a form and meaning, we can speak of culture.

In culture, human consciousness is revealed along with the 'products' resulting from it such as fields, technology, and worship.

Ortner's thesis, also held by others, is that women are identified with that which each culture finds less interesting and less valuable than itself, namely, with nature in the most general sense of the word.

Culture is a process of giving shape and meaning by which humanity surpasses the data of natural existence, transcends it, bends it to its own purposes, and dominates it in service of its interests. Culture becomes an expression of human consciousness and considers itself different from and also superior to nature.

This latter is based on its ability to transform nature and to 'socialize' it (Ortner 1974, p. 73).

Those wanting to keep things clear can hold on to the dualism: man as symbol of culture, woman as symbol of nature. But Ortner warns us against simplifications and develops the thesis further. Women are thought of as *closer to* nature than men. This implies that culture recognizes that women are also involved in its processes but at the same time remain more deeply rooted in nature. I will follow here Ortner's nuanced investigation, in which she poses questions on three levels.

The first is the physiological level. Woman's body is regarded as closer to nature. Woman leads the life of the 'species', while man is free to take up his cultural tasks. Woman is supplied with organs unnecessary for her own individual life, the functioning of which is sometimes painful or troublesome (I am thinking here of the menstrual cycle). These organs are there to create new human life. Sharply put, the female body is there to reproduce life in each generation; while men, who do not have this function, express themselves by forming and creating in the external world. Men make (art) objects which stand up to time (transcendence), and women 'only' produce new life, thus 'more of the same'. Simone de Beauvoir in her book *Le deuxième Sexe* introduced the term 'immanence' to describe woman's existence.

In this light, we can also 'understand' why male activity such as killing, in hunting and in war, is of more significance in in public life than woman's bearing new life. For, as de Beauvoir concludes, not the giving of life but the risking of life raises man above the animal. Therefore the sex which kills is more important than the sex which gives birth! The woman's reproductive ability implies endless repetition. The man's creative ability is goal-project-orientated and surpasses the 'natural' (de Beauvoir, cited in Ortner 1974, p. 75).

Yet women also have a fully human consciousness, and participate in projects which surpass nature. Fate will have it, Ortner says, that they have for the most part accepted the male culture's attributed and imposed limitations, and in so doing have kept their lower status. The result is that 'woman' is felt to be a sort of link, an intermediary, between nature and culture, and thus lower on the scale of transcendence than 'man' (Ortner 1974, p. 76).

We now come to the second level: woman's social role is also seen as closer to nature. Woman's 'natural' production, as opposed to man's 'art-ificial' creation, also has social implications. Precisely her physiological functions and their concrete expression limit a woman's mobility in social life. I am thinking here not only of carrying bearing and nursing new life, but also of taking care of it. For this she has to stay at home, although recent study has shown that this is not true of all cultures.

This means that 'home' also receives the *label* 'natural', in contrast to public life which is culture's domain. For this reason, children up to puberty are associated with nature. Initiation rites in many societies complete the passage, especially for boys, from nature to culture, to 'real life'.

This contrast has still other aspects, namely, the opposition between 'home' and 'outside world', or 'private' and 'public' (to put it in modern terms). It is clear that women in their care and education of children also contribute to their socialization, and thus also perform a cultural role. But this is seen as restricted to the home and is thus of a limited, lower level of importance. Men (the fathers of other men) introduce their sons to public life and cultural thought.

To make the whole even more complicated: even when practical everyday activities are concerned, there are still differences to note depending on *who* performs them. For example, each day women cook meals and perform not only an exclusively natural act (feeding), but also a cultural act, processing and transforming natural products and resources into food. But it is generally known that when *haute cuisine* is involved as an expression of a country's culture (e.g. France's), the cook is almost always male, taking a central place and, moreover, a clearer position in (semi-)public life.

Women therefore also occupy an intermediary position in social relationships, linking 'nature' and 'culture' (Ortner, 80).

Finally, there is the level of the woman's psyche: the traditional roles attributed to woman on the basis of her physique also give her a psychic structure different from the male's. This mentality is also seen as closer to nature. Here we touch a delicate point which feminists question. Ortner therefore hastens to say that she does not mean that this is a congenital difference. Following Nancy Chodorow's research, she wants to show that this 'feminine' psyche is brought about in all cultures by women's experience in the dominant socialization process.

One of the dimensions of this socialization process that is encountered nearly everywhere is the opposition between the concrete and the abstract: the 'female' personality is more involved with concrete feelings, affairs and people than with abstract matters. She also tends to become more involved with personal and individual situations. In the second place, and clearly connected with the first, there is the dimension of greater subjectivity as opposed to objectivity. While men represent their experiences of self, others, space, and time in an individualistic, objective and detached manner, women express their experiences in a relatively interpersonal, subjective and direct manner (cf. Gilligan 1982, passim).

More interesting than the observation of these dimensions is the conclusion that they again confirm the cultural view of women as closer to nature. Ortner appeals here to a publication by Chodorow where it is observed that these psychic differences have nothing to do with genetic programming, but everything to do with family structure (Chodorow 1974). It is primarily the woman who is responsible for the care of children and the later socialization of, in particular, the daughters. Moreover, the structural situation of child-rearing, strengthened by male and female role modelling, produces the differences, which are then reflected and reproduced in the sociology of the sexes in their adult lives.

Chodorow asserts that in early youth, children develop a personal identification with the mother, with her personality, values, behaviour and attitude. But for the son, this is true for only a limited time, until he turns to a male role identity and thus an identification with the father. Since in many families the father is often absent, this construction of an identification with the father implies more a 'positional identification', in other words, more an identification with the father's *position* than with the father as a personal individual. The daughter is more likely to continue without shocks to learn her female identity, which she sees represented in her mother. Girls seem to become adults with a greater sense of connectedness, given their closeness to their mother, while boys have to adapt themselves to a male world and have to 'learn' roles. The woman's status looks more 'natural', while boys have to prove they have become adult men. Herein lies the break. Accomplishments have to be demonstrated. Ortner speaks of 'achieved and ascribed status', status based on accomplishments (for the male) and status based on attribution (for the female). This latter is viewed as 'more natural'.

The model set before the girl prepares her for her role in adult life when her children in turn have to reach a personal identification with her. This forms an endless cycle. Precisely this repetition leads, on the level of cultural meaning – that is the position women are assigned in relation to the world – to the way they are seen more as 'nature', i.e. as immanent and imbedded in the course of given things rather than as 'culture' which invites transcendence of these givens. Women tend more to begin direct and immediate relations, while men often to a greater degree have relations with intermediary categories and groups than with persons or objects themselves.

The term 'intermediary' in this regard has already been used with various meanings. First of all, it means simply a 'middle status' in a hierarchy of nature and culture. Next it includes 'mediation', as in the case of education, when the mother transposes 'nature' into 'culture' in the family milieu. This becomes very important as a stabilizing factor in a given culture. There is, therefore, a social pressure on her 'mediation' in terms of reinforcing traditions which strongly limit her in the personal form she gives her life. This also affects the sexual activities she is permitted. These are generally much more strictly regulated for women than for men. This also affects the limitations which drastically reduce her participation in the events of public life. But due in part to all these factors, women are nearly everywhere socialized to such a degree that they demonstrate more conservative attitudes, opinions and behaviour.

And finally, this 'intermediary' position is also coloured by a greater ambiguity. Women are felt to be living on the edge, on the border between nature and culture. They do not belong completely to either the one or the other. They are restricted when culture is involved and are praised when they fulfil the role imposed on them. They are simultaneously tempting *and* confusing (and therefore something threatening) in their blossoming corporality, but polluting through menstrual blood. They are necessary for their reproductive abilities, but non-existent when cultural, political and social responsibilities are involved (Ortner, 85).

M. Z. Rosaldo notes that in many societies women, in contrast with men, are often viewed as anomalies, as deviant and 'irregular'. They live and work in such a way that they scarcely participate in the laws and arrangements constructed and imposed by men. The result is that, from a male viewpoint, they stand outside these social and cultural arrangements. Men count because they operate in all ranks, classes and functions; women are only women. They are important for their 'mothering', and from it they derive their power which, however, has no part to play in the formal aspects of power in the male world (Rosaldo 1974, pp. 31ff.).

It is clear that many women in various societies find themselves caught in a vicious circle. Several aspects of a woman's situation contribute to her being seen as closer to nature (among which her physical 'equipment' is of first importance). Precisely this being closer to nature is incorporated into institutional forms which reproduce her situation. When we search for a solution, this vicious circle reappears: a new cultural attribution of meaning to women can only arise in another, a new, social reality, but this new social reality can only grow from a differently coloured cultural outlook.

I do not want to say the situation is hopeless and without prospects. On the contrary! In many countries in Western society, and also outside it, we see changes taking place. Movement is visible, and that is a positive signal.

2

I must provide a few notes on the preceding section of this chapter, challenged as I am by the critical remarks of cultural anthropologists such as Carol MacCormack. She wants to add a second opinion to the cultural analysis of Ortner and others, in order to include the necessary distinctions.

From her analysis I would like to note the following two important points:

a. MacCormack warns against making contrasts too rigid, such as nature and culture, and against considering them as rigid antitheses. There seem to be many means of transition where we see how nature is made into culture by assigning it meaning and rules (e.g. incest taboo within marriages). The structuralists from Levi-Strauss's well-known school have shown us the human ability to make binary distinctions, i.e. the ability of the human mind to construct observations of the surrounding world by seeing antitheses and contrasts: light cannot be observed without knowing darkness.

To the extent that more of these observations are collected in contrasts (e.g. soul and body, reason and emotion), analogies are sought among the various pairs, and classifications are formed. But even though these binary contrasts are vital for human thought, they remain symbolic structures, trying to organize observed reality; but they have only a relative value since they cannot capture reality. In empirical research, this reality appears to be much more complicated as well as more fluid ... The observed phenomena are, in the end, more real than the symbols, and not the reverse. Therefore, the opposition of nature and culture can be a factor in classifying phenomena; but it must not become a timeless, unchangeable, and a normative model, as if there were no diversity in cultures and in the assignment of meaning, not to mention historical development! (MacCormack 1980, pp, 1–6).

b. Next, Rosaldo warns against another but associated misconception. It is not an imaginary danger that data from cultural anthropological research are misused by being taken as a universal reality apart from their historical context. Anthropology cannot express universal human truth, and the data from research cannot be used to formulate modern political demands.

We pursue a dead-end road when we think that looking for our origins will help to advance women, because we then forget that people are, to an important degree, the product of our history and of our modern world. The same holds true for sexual asymmetry. If this was an unchangeable given, then we could forget all hope of change. The forms which sex takes in the various cultures and in the various historical periods have to be explained in social and political terms. What we need to do first of all is to look at the relation between men and women and at each one's opportunities in order to explain on this basis how their interests, lifestyles and image-formations have become opposed (Rosaldo 1980, *passim*).

In this study I am concerned with this image-formation. It is striking that however many historical and cultural differences arise, the image of women up to the present day is clearly related to corporality and 'nature', and that men are associated with culture.

We will meet these images several times more, and each time will find that we have to do with more than one meaning of the term 'nature'. This makes the whole even more complicated. But the image, the 'mental picture', remains.

2

'MOTHER' NATURE

This chapter treats of the far-reaching changes which took place bettween 1500 and 1700 in the human experience of nature. In section 1 I deal with the characteristics and aspects of nature as experienced organically, and then in section 2 I consider the results of the change when nature became increasingly thought of mechanically: the transition from the image of an organism to that of a machine. These results are important not only for nature itself, but also for women.

A well-known figure on whose work this transition has left its mark is Francis Bacon. In section 3 I look more closely at the significance of what he says.

1

For millennia people experienced nature as a great mystery. They lived in its midst but lived in trepidation of all that surrounded them and of everything upon which they felt dependent. The earth, the mountains, the woods; the seas and rivers; the universe with its wind and clouds; the planets; the order of day and night, ebb and flow; the alternating seasons; they were all mysteries within which people lived, mysteries which fascinated them, and before which they shuddered as before powers greater than themselves. Humanity felt itself a part of nature; included in it, but smaller than nature; in its debt, but not passive before it.

From the very beginning people intervened in nature, making homes for themselves in it, leaving traces of their passage on it, wandering, seeking food and finally cultivating it, establishing themselves and creating their own civilization.

Their trembling before nature and the cosmos also led to the first religious experiences, to religion and ritual, to veneration of super-human powers and forces which enlivened the cosmos, giving it order and regularity and guaranteeing fertility. In particular for this last, in all the different religions nature was looked upon as feminine, and the earth was addressed as Mother. On this point there was even no change when biblical revelation introduced the concept of creation and proclaimed a new vision of earth and nature.

Nature was personified as woman, as a noble Lady, Mother Nature, as a wise woman or as a queen ruling over all. Nature's variety and laws expressed the forces living in her. In particular, nature as the nurturing mother, the earth which gives life but also takes it back, are the images we meet most often. They show that nature was experienced as a living organism.

What we will now observe, during the centuries, but especially and very explicitly between *c.* 1500 and 1700 in our Western cultural history, is the transposition of an organic view of nature towards a mechanical view. For this description I have followed, for the most part, the reliable study by Carolyn Merchant, *The Death of Nature*.

By an organic view, we mean a view and experience of nature as a dynamic, creative and ordering principle that causes phenomena in the material world to be, as well as causing their movement and development, their birth and death. The term 'organic' normally refers to bodily organs, to the structure and composition of living things. Organic implies that life, movement and growth occurs from within. The term 'organicism' refers to the teaching that organic structure is the result of a character or a force present in and part of material.

A mechanical view of nature, on the other hand, refers to an influencing or even a domination by external forces, to the machine, the instrumentarium, to technology. Instead of independence and spontaneous growth, we see the external control of nature by mechanical tools and positive sciences (Merchant 1980, p. xx). In addition to the positive image of the earth and nature as caring mother, there is also a negative view of nature as something unpredictable, whimsical and chaotic. That was also a real aspect of human experience. The transition to the first scientific revolution had an unmistakable influence on both these images. The positive image of the nurturing mother disappears in the background when rationalism and mechanization push ahead; and the negative image of the 'wild' and unpredictable nature gives way as humanity exercises power and domination over it.

We can easily assume that human intervention in nature is by no means a 'modern' problem, but a question as old as the act of intervening. In many old Mediterranean civilizations, hillside mining (and the related deforestation) was known. Respect for nature still curbed it and questioned whether it was necessary. The mother's body should not be mutilated to extract gold from her innards! In most traditional cultures it was supposed that minerals and metals had to ripen in Mother Earth's womb. The mines were compared to the vagina. Through metallurgy, the birth of the living metal was hastened in the artificial womb of the oven – it was an abortion, a premature operation in the metal's natural growth cycle (Merchant 1980, p. 4).

Pliny (AD 23–79) noted in his *Natural History* (cited in Merchant 1980, p. 30) that there was a reason why the earth preserved deep in her womb treasures not intended for people and kept them hidden there. Earthquakes were an expression of her indignation when she was violated deep in her womb. Pliny argued that the product of mining led only to greed (gold); or to human cruelty, when it concerned iron shaped into weapons.

Agricola (sixteenth century) repeats this argument in his *De Re Metallica* when he points to the treasure trove of spices and plants that Mother Earth has produced and to our aggression when people still want to conquer her hidden treasures. He mentions the danger that the balance in nature will be disturbed and broken if it is plundered without limit. Even then there was discussion of water pollution, e.g. the river Arno near Florence and the spoiled environment for the fish! (Merchant 1980, pp. 31–6). Another significant argument is found in John Milton's *Paradise Lost* (1667), when he suggests that mining not only results in the sin of greed, but that it also leads to a second great sin, human lust, by which he means digging and rooting about in 'female flesh'. If one poet had objected to this, a colleague, John Donne (1573–1631), had no such inhibitions in expressing his pleasure in it. In his own Elegy XIX, 'To His Mistress Going to Bed', he describes voluptuously the delight of claiming the newly conquered land on the American continent, and its exploration on all sides: 'Let my roving hands find their way before, behind, between, above, below . . .' (Merchant 1980, pp. 40–1).

These lines need no explanation; the earth, here the newly discovered land, is a woman, delightful to possess, to touch, to dis-cover.

These references are but a few examples from the many that could be given. They are sufficient to show that the feeling for nature, the interventions in it and the ethical reflections about it are in a period of change. Although concern for nature itself as well as for humanity's relation to it (greed, cruelty and lust) were dominant at first, the urge for conquest, for profit, and the desire to possess, were gradually victorious.

2

The changes taking place here in imagery and attitudes did not appear from thin air, but owe their existence to the historical, social and economic movements taking place in various European countries. Although the accent in this chapter will be put primarily on the *changing* and mechanization of nature, I want first to point out the characteristics of a society still satisfied with an organic view of its environment. Only then can we understand the radical results of the transition to another period.

Merchant notes that there is always a connection between the experience of the individual 'self' and its own society (both being microcosms) and the greater, all-encompassing whole, the macrocosm. The changes entering history in times of transition exert their influence on all three levels. For this reason I wish to pause here briefly in order to clarify the transition from the organic theory of nature to a mechanistic theory.

Our starting-point is the medieval and Renaissance view of nature and society in which there was an organic analogy between the human body (microcosm) and the greater world (macrocosm).

Within this there are variants as follows:
– The first variant is that there is an observed hierarchical order in the cosmos and in society which coincides with the organic relation of the parts of the body. It is possible to to speak here of a projection of humanness on to the cosmos. The term 'nature' involves both the inborn character and talent of people and animals as well as the creative force active in material objects and phenomena.
– A second image was based on nature as an active unity of opposites related in a dialectical tension.
– A third possibility was the Arcadian image of nature as

beneficent, pleasant, peaceful and rural. It was named after Arcadia, the rural heart of Greek Peloponnesos.

Each of these images and interpretations had a different social implication. The first was a justification of the existing social order. The second justified the changes in society towards a new and more democratic ideal. The third justified the escape from the problems in urban life by a return to pleasant landscapes, to 'nature'.

In this last case nature was still an attractive feminine form; but it was passive and intended only to supply rest to overtired men who wanted to relax from the tensions of the market. In both art and literature we can find numerous representations of this (Merchant 1980, p. 6).

We have used the word 'market' as a symbol for the transition from the earlier small-scale economy of farmers and craftspeople, organized to benefit their own lives, to a world-scale economy, a world market based on profit, capital and supply. Meanwhile, technical development had not stood still. Large-scale coal-mining and ship-building endeavours provided the opportunity to undertake distant travels, to conquer other continents, and to trade. The destruction of forests (wood for ships!) and the draining of swamps, to give a few examples, caused an ecological crisis, in several parts of seventeenth century England, similar to our own in all but size.

After describing all these incisive changes and developments, Merchant lists three variations found in the organic theory of society that are important in the understanding of the transition from organism to mechanism. If the triplet mentioned above started from the differences to be noted in the understanding of nature and with the consequences they imply for a view of society, the starting-point now is the experience of a changing society and of the tension caused by the influence organic thought can still exert in it.

Her three variations are as follows:
– The first is based on the medieval view of society as a hierarchy. The political structure has as its metaphorical model the organic unity of the human body. As a rigid pattern of status groups, this variant represented a conservative view of the social order corresponding to the experiences of the feudal lords and the medieval Church.

– The second variant was aimed at levelling this hierarchy and is based on the experiences of the village community.

– Finally, there is the revolutionary version of the organic theory, which defended the complete overthrow of all social hierarchies. This was the symbol of the utopian aspiration to replace the established order with an egalitarian community in which it would be possible to return to the 'golden age' of harmony with nature.

It is clear that the word 'organic', when used to describe an organic society, an organic community and an organic utopia, receives each time another accent and a change of meaning.

In an organic model of a hierarchically structured society, each part of nature and society had its own place, laws, duties and values. All this contributed to the perfection of the whole universal community in which the 'lower' was there to serve the 'higher', while the purpose of the 'higher' was to lead the 'lower'. The apex of this model was the monarchy, which linked the political order to the cosmic order. The medieval sovereign represented God in temporal, worldly matters. The Church did the same spiritual affairs. For the philosopher Nicholas of Cusa (fifteenth century), the Church was the body of God. The clergy was its soul, while God was the all-pervasive unifying Spirit.

This order is clearly static in construction and in operation. Each thing knows its place and stays there. It is striking that the metaphor of the human body recurs frequently when organic structures are discussed, and appears to play an important role (Merchant 1980, pp. 69ff.).

A well-known example can be found in John of Salisbury's *Policraticus* (1159). The social body was endowed with life and ruled by reason in the form of the prince who functioned, along with the clergy, as its soul. Those representing the provinces were the senses – the ears, eyes and tongue. The senate was the heart. One hand bore weapons and defended the citizens against external aggression; the other, without weapons, took care of internal discipline. Financial experts were the stomach and intestines. They were ordered to care for good health by keeping the economy flowing (Merchant 1980, p. 70).

In the second version also, the organic society model, the community's well-being had precedence over that of each separate individual; but it was the community itself, and not a superimposed authority, which formulated principles and decisions and had the right to choose its own leader. Here, too, the whole was greater than the sum of the parts, but these parts were far more equal to one another.

The need for revolution felt by some farmers and craftspeople was expressed in organic utopias. The new society they desired would free them from the tyrannical slavery of political and religious overlords, and would ground common ownership in a government characterized by brotherhood. There would be a new unique revelation from God. It would be immanent in nature and therefore a truly spiritual religion, no longer denigrating nature but elevating it to the status of a divinely creative force.

Campanella (1568–1639), the author of these ideas, wrote his utopian *The City of the Sun* in Naples, where labour unrest dominated. Andrea followed him with a second utopian work, *Christianopolis*, where he also pleaded for a more equal distribution of wealth based on an original harmony between people and nature. Holistic sounds reverberate here!

Thus we see that technological progress and its resulting economic developments and expansion changed people's lives and thinking, that social movements undermined the organic hierarchical order, and that the earth's womb and the resources belonging to all became the basis for an intensive market economy. There is more. Like this human microcosm, the macrocosm was also transformed. Whereas previously the projection of the 'self' and society on the heavenly bodies allowed the macrocosm to be experienced as a tightly interwoven unity of body, soul and spirit held together in a hierarchical order, *now* all these elements underwent a thorough reorganization and change or else they were even rejected completely by the mechanistic framework which was becoming ever more dominant. We find the results of this change in the writings of diverse philosophical schools, each of which tried in its own way to describe and explain humanity, the world and the cosmos. Organic features gradually disappeared from nature (at least in mainstream thinking; dissidents remained vocal) to make room for mechanically described components as a sign of the scientific revolution. Together with the changes taking placed in both societal and ecclesiastical spheres (the Reformation!), these new situations and ways of thinking ruptured humankind's unity with nature, causing uncertainty, insecurity and anxiety.

The Copernican discovery, which removed the earth from its central place and ordered the cosmos around the sun, further underlined this feeling of insecurity. The well-ordered structure in which people had lived was in disarray. Nature and society became chaotic and threatening, and humankind's lot became unpredictable and violent. It became necessary to 'subdue' all this, and to dominate it.

The question now is: What was the woman's place in these times of disorder? Generally stated, she was thought to be closer to nature, even in its aspects of unpredictability, 'wildness' and chaos. It was therefore even more necessary to make her subject to man's reason and authority. Moreover, she was attributed with a greater sexual urge and emotion, and therefore, just as with nature, she had to be forcefully kept in her place. Woman's sexual greed and desire harmed the man's body! It was this desire that linked her to evil, to the devil, and was one of the basic elements of the large-scale witch hunts in these centuries.

At the heart of the frenzy expressed in the witch hunts, the merciless hunt for black slaves and the extermination of Native Americans (to give just few examples), lay men's boundless pride in general, and that of white Western European men in particular. To this were added the repressed and suppressed but aggressive fear of female sexuality as well as the greed to accumulate capital at the expense of the indigenous inhabitants of a conquered continent.

In this time of continuing industrialization, of economic and technological development, we note not only large-scale affronts against women, but also their gradual and systematic withdrawal from public life to their 'place', at home in the family. In the pre-industrial, organic, hierarchical society, many women derived their role and place from the class to which, through their marriage, they belonged. There were also women in more humble strata of society who had a productive role in the agricultural industry and in the urban retail trade. But *now* the dominant male culture forced them into their 'natural' milieu. Women went back from production to reproduction. Whereas women had had a considerable position in the area of midwifery, they now had to give way to the more technically equipped male doctors (Merchant 1980, pp. 141–8).

The tendency, arising from changes in all areas of life, to dominate nature as well as woman and the 'female' is clearly exemplified in the person and work of Francis Bacon (1561–1626). He is one of the famous 'founding fathers' of modern science. His writings reflect the changed thought on nature as well as on women. His use of languages and style, and the metaphors he chooses, give an unmistakable reflection of these changes.

Bacon lived from 1561 until 1626, and was an eminent thinker and scientist who ushered in a new period. He was a member of parliament and thereafter filled numerous high political positions, including being attorney general to the British high court at the time when James I stiffened the laws against witchcraft. Bacon was thus no stranger to this phenomenon. His whole life was filled with the desire to bring renewal and change to English society. He was initially very practically orientated in this pursuit, wanting not so much a new philosophy as above all a new England.

He aimed at increasing the well-being of the people and at the elimination of the poverty in which they lived. Even more, he wanted to lead the way in creating abundance by subjecting nature to the needs of humanity. In this context, too, he used the images of fertilization and procreation (Farrington 1964, pp. 16–17). Bacon only started writing late in life, when he discovered that he had to support his ideas on the needed renewal with the force of arguments. One of his first (brief) works is *The Male Birth of Time* (1602–3), the theme of which is the interpretation of nature. Its subtitle is *The Great Restoration of Man's Power Over the Universe*. It starts with a prayer to God in which Bacon asks that everything in the human mind clouded by superstition and folly be removed. He hoped a brighter light would be given to him so that he could interpret with maximum clarity the book of nature (existing beside the book of God's revelation, the Bible).

Bacon's only wish was to expand the regretfully narrow boundaries of man's power over the universe (by 'power' he referred to the *dominium terrae*, the 'subdue the earth' of Genesis 1, to which I will return in Part 2). Here Bacon made the transition from 'imitating' nature (organic thinking in terms of humanity, society and cosmos) to 'dominating' it (Farrington 1964, p. 27). As a scientist, he was orientated towards the light of nature and not the 'darkness of classical antiquity' (Farrington 1964, p. 48).

Using sensory perceptions, Bacon wanted to observe closely all the phenomena of nature. In this way he introduced the empirical method, that is, the posing of specific questions whose answers were to be arrived at by experimentation. He rejected preconceived hypotheses. His method was inductive: discover facts, order them, then deduce from them knowledge of natural laws. Nature had to be 'interpreted'.

In complete agreement with the social reforms which reduced women to psychological and reproductive tools, Bacon developed the power of language into a political instrument to reduce the 'feminine' nature to a tool of economic production. This 'feminine' metaphor became an instrument to forge scientific knowledge and method into human power over nature. Both his period's ambivalence towards women and the interrogation of witches penetrated Bacon's description of nature through his style of imagery and contributed to making the earth, once a nurturing mother and the womb of life, into a source of secrets to be unveiled for the general benefit of humankind and for economic progress.

Women were regarded as closer to nature and in tune with its quirks and secrets. In the pact they were accused of making with the devil, the demonic character of these natural forces and the sexuality of the 'witches' came together. It is therefore not surprising that there is a parallel between the language used both to describe the tortures for extracting secrets from witches and to discuss the method of discovering nature's secrets. In his *De Dignitate et Augmentis Scientiarum* (1623), Bacon wrote:

> The way in which witchcraft, magic, and all such superstitions are prosecuted and run aground . . . not only sheds useful light on how people accused of such things should be treated, but we can also borrow from it useful directions for unveiling nature's secrets. No one need have scruples about penetrating these caverns and corners when interrogating the truth is his only object. (cited in Merchant 1980, p. 168)

He encouraged the scientist to subdue nature, to enslave it, and to shape it with mechanical techniques. In this way its intrigues and secrets would be discovered.

In another of his works, *Novum Organon* (1620), Bacon argued: 'The new interrogation method leads to the analysis and dismemberment of nature. The spirit provides the suggestions and the hands do the work. In this way human knowledge and human power are one' (cited in Merchant 1980, p. 171).

This led Bacon to conclude that humanity, through the power of its knowledge and science, regained the dominance over nature it had lost through original sin. Whereas a woman's curiosity had caused the fall of humanity from the power God had given, *now* the merciless inquisition of another woman, nature, is used to regain this power.

Bacon referred to this restoration of the power God had given humanity in his earliest work, *The Male Birth of Time: The Great Restoration of Man's Power Over the Universe*. It was not published during his life. Farrington's English edition dates from 1964. The subtitle summarizes Bacon's conclusion that what up until then had been called science, even that of ancient Greek philosophers, proclaimed error and led humanity along a dead-end road. That is why it produced weak fruit, only daughters. Bacon believed the science of the 'ancients' had failed because 'it wanted to create a universe of the human spirit'. The arrogant assumption of the Creator's role was punished with infertility. He calls this a female failure. But this science is also impotent (male!) and incapable of creating virile successors. Now we see where Bacon is leading. Humanity must first make its spirit submissive and receptive to God's truth. Then it can be pure and chaste (the spirit becomes female here), and only then can it produce a male, virile science. Only when the spirit is made receptive to God, can God transform it into a forceful, potent, virile instrument with which to relate to nature.

The transformation of the spirit from female to male is seen clearly in the structure of Bacon's writing here. The first part is a prayer addressed to God; in the second part an adult scientist addresses his son, a virile successor. From that moment, nature is indisputably female, the object passed on from father to son. Here we find Bacon's well-known statement: 'In truth, I have come to bring you nature and all her children, that you may have her serve you and be your slave' (Farrington 1964, p. 62). He now makes his son his heir, who will expand the regrettable confines of human domination over the universe to the limits of what can be expected. Now Bacon's accent is like that of God himself, and he passes on his task to *his* son . . .

Bacon was convinced the scientific method, when combined with mechanical technology, would create a 'new organ', a new research system, that would unite knowledge with material power. Technical inventions, such as the printing press, gunpowder, and the magnet,

> help us to think about the secrets still enclosed in nature's bosom. They exercise more than a gentle leadership over nature, they have the power to conquer and subject it, to shake it to its foundations. . . . [Under influence of mechanical techniques] nature betrays its secrets more completely. (Farrington 1964, pp. 93–9)

Merchant concludes:

> The interrogation of witches as symbol for the interrogation of nature; the hall of justice as model for its inquisition; mechanized torture as an instrument to repress chaos, were fundamentally important for the scientific method as power. For Bacon and others, sexual policy contributed to structuring the character of the empirical method, which would produce a new kind of knowledge as well as a new ideology of objectivity, apparently totally devoid of cultural and political presuppositions. (Merchant 1980, p. 172)

In 1624, shortly before his death, Francis Bacon also penned a utopian work, *New Atlantis*. His view of the ideal society was definitely different from those of his predecessors, Campanella and Andrea, who wished for an organic, egalitarian society in which women and men were more or less equal. Bacon's ideal structure was a hierarchical, patriarchal society modelled on the early modern patriarchal family. In this family structure the father entered the great hall first, followed by his male descendants, and then by his female descendants. Although the mother was present, she was set apart behind a glass screen where she could sit without being seen. Bacon put scientists on the highest level of the hierarchically ordered utopian city and state. In their hands lay progress and power for the general well-being. His scientists, dressed in a costly black coat with white lining, assumed the form of a priesthood empowered to free (absolve) humanity from all human misery.

In *New Atlantis* Bacon seems to promote the creation of new organs rather than the enjoyment and respect of what already exists. The scientists in 'Solomon's House', as their residence is called in Bacon's utopia, not only produce new forms of birds, and animals, but also create new types, of plants and species. They also experiment to find out what is applicable to the human body. Francis Bacon, a modern scientist . . .

That is one side of the coin. The other should also be examined. The transition from an organic to a mechanical experience of nature finds obvious expression in the metaphors Mother Nature uses in her reaction to human behaviour. First, Mother Earth complains that her womb was violently penetrated; in a later period we hear Mother Nature lamenting that her modest apparel was rent by unjust and violent male brutality. After the scientific revolution, a French sculptor portrayed her timorously removing her veil and offering herself to science. From active mentor and mother, she has become a spiritless and subordinated body. The new mechanical order, which would result in nature's death, had begun (Merchant 1980, ch. 7, *passim*).

As is clear from the foregoing, the process of allaying the fear of chaos had its unmistakable influence on the seventeenth century. The new mechanical philosophy put the cosmos, society and the 'self' on the same level by using a new metaphor, the machine. Whereas before, in an organic world, 'order' meant the functioning of each part within a larger whole in accordance with its own nature, *now* 'order' has become the predictable behaviour of each sub-element in a rationally determined system of laws. Because nature is now considered to be a system of parts to be examined, moved by external instead of internally living forces, this mechanical setting easily legitimizes the manipulation of nature.

The mechanical, objective philosophies formulated by Descartes and others put ideas about order, domination and manipulation higher than those which took change, uncertainty and unpredictability into consideration.

Up to that time, many thinkers believed in a divine world soul, an expression of God's immanence in 'his' creation; now this soul became a mechanism of and in the world. God became merely the one who made all this in some remote past.

Of course, discussion continued between proponents and

opponents of the new way of thinking, but the mechanical metaphor for an ordered society continued. This mechanism became the expression of growing human power and of technology itself. It is interesting to note how temperance, the virtue of moderation, is increasingly seen as the symbol of *measure*. While the middle ages still portrayed moderation as Lady Temperance, pouring water into the wine vessel, in the fourteenth century she is given a compass and a mechanical clock (Merchant 1980, p. 223).

World and cosmos are increasingly seen as a perfect technical clock. God is assigned a minimal role. 'He' is the one who, once upon a time, wound up the clock which has continued ticking ever since. Practical results of this mechanical way of looking at things, deforestation, air pollution, and other ailments, led to protests from those pleading for a greater role for God in nature and creation and for a better management of nature. I return to this in Chapter 5.

3

MAN-AGING NATURE

We were able to note in the previous chapter that the entry of a new, 'modern' natural science, and the opposing view of nature as a research object to be dominated, brought all-pervasive changes to the experience and appreciation of nature, but equally to that of women. Bacon's image-rich language speaks volumes!

In this chapter, nature is again discussed; this time as the object of rational thought and research. After reflecting in section 1 on the Greek word for nature, *physis*, and its continuing effect, we turn in section 2 to Descartes, the philosopher of rationalism, a tendency in philosophy rooted in the reason's ability to make distinctions, which has thoroughly determined scientific thinking. Section 3 closes the chapter with a look at the consequences of rationalism, including those for our own time.

1

While Bacon's approach and school led to the tendency we call 'empiricism', in practically the same period in France, Descartes' work led to 'rationalism'. Empiricism put all its emphasis on human observation and experience, and was orientated primarily towards practical research. Rationalism put thought, reason and the process of acquiring knowledge under the spotlight. Both trends completed humanity's separation from nature. As Bacon sees it, this is still an I–thou relationship, but one of power and domination over 'Mother' Nature; for Descartes, the relation between the thinking person and nature has become an I–it relation.

It is a characteristic of our Western culture that when we speak of 'nature' we nearly always do so in terms of opposites. Nature is, for example, set opposite 'spirit' in the division of natural sciences and arts; we have already examined the usual nature versus culture division in Chapter 1.

Things have not always been this way. To demonstrate this I

would like to give a short excursus on Greek philosophy, to trace the original meaning of the Greek word for nature, *physis*. In Book VIII of his *Physics*, Aristotle looks at all that happens as a unity, and attributes all causality in this unity to one single force, Nature. Nature links the multiplicity of things, relating them to one another and establishing order. It is also the principle of all motion in the world. *Physis* is more a principle of unity at the basis of the whole universe. To the essence of *physis* belongs all that moves, that is, all that arises from the hidden, what is, and what perishes. Nature as *physis* includes: all things temporal; the whole, as well as all the parts; words, extra-human matters and human nature; the soul causing movement, and even the gods.

The only things outside nature are the realities which escape time's cycle of starting and perishing: the immovable mover (Aristotle's name for God), as well as fate, to which the gods also are subject. But everything that is, is in time and through time; and therefore, as 'becoming' or 'perishing', is *physis*.

This view implied that humanity could not be outside nature, but was regulated within it. The human soul was an image of the soul of the cosmos, the world soul. The ellipse is the basic shape in *physis*, portraying the process of becoming–being–perishing (being hidden).

G. Liedke, from whom I have borrowed this description, points out that something important happens when Greek *physis* is translated into Latin *natura* (Liedke 1979, pp. 36ff.). Every translation is an interpretation revealing the translator's context. The Roman poet Lucretius translated the Greek didactic poem *Peri Physeos* by Empedocles with *De Rerum natura(e)*. Two changes take place here: (1) *natura* from the root *nasci* (to be born, to arise) has no element referring to 'perishing'. (2) The word *rerum* is added, the genitive plural of *res* (matters or things at one's disposal). *Res* is a juridical concept for the Romans, and includes affairs over which one has power. The Latin translation of *physis* means the origin of that over which one has power (Liedke 1979, p. 38 cites G. Picht, *Der Begriff der Natur und seine Geschichte*. The concept of nature as something which allows all that is to perish was foreign to the Romans. The 'arising' remained, but the perishing disappeared. It is hardly necessary to argue that this situation greatly influenced our present Western concept of nature which has abandoned the Greek cyclical aspect.

If we look back now to the Greek *physis* concept, we can see that Greek thinking distinguishes between what repeatedly generates and perishes (e.g. plants), and its unchangeable being. This unchangeable is the divine, permanent being, a being which also belongs to and appears in the *physis*.

This way of thinking differs from the traditional Judeo-Christian belief in creation which rejects the idea that God, in one way or another, is part of nature. The biblical creation stories remove nature from the divine sphere; the world is profane. This creation theology and its results will be treated extensively in Part 2, but we can note here that this desacralization of nature also diminished respect for nature.

Two other factors are also important for understanding the Western view of nature: (1) we note a surprising technological development and progress, even among the ancients (aqueducts, obelisks), and (2) Greco-Roman antiquity lacked a systematic planning which would allow the scientific results they discovered to be used and developed technically.

This latter can, of course, have to do with not wanting to interfere too often in holy nature, but this attitude would be more applicable to the Greeks than to the Romans. A more readily available explanation for this gap between technical development and their great discoveries in natural science is the minimal value attributed to labour as such. Manual labour was not highly regarded, for the Greeks it was the same as slave labour. Free time, *scholē*, was the valuable element for the free citizen, who kept busy with art, philosophy and politics (Liedke 1979, pp. 40ff.). In Christianity, we do not meet this denigration of labour. We only have to think of the cultivation and all the forms of cultural labour performed by the monks in Western Europe to understand that during the centuries before the technological revolution radical changes took place upon which theoreticians of the early modern period, such as Bacon and Descartes, could build. Radical changes do not occur spontaneously, but are gradually prepared for in history. We already see, in any case, a change in human thinking and behaviour towards nature and our environment: nature as *physis* (Greeks) becomes nature as possession (Romans); then nature as creation, in which manual labour is positively evaluated as an expression of a creative task. A second aspect of this change, where nature

is altered from an organic whole to a mechanical system, was
treated in Chapter 2.

2

I now return to rationalism. To understand better its meaning, we
need to pause to look at the person and work of the philosopher
René Descartes (1595–1650). His well-known work *Discours de la
Méthode*, published in Leiden in 1639 (he had lived there since
1629), explains how in his research in and study of physics he
reached new insights and conclusions, conclusions far distant
from those of customary speculative philosophy. Descartes
wanted to find a practical philosophy

> which would teach us the force and method of fire, water, air,
> the stars and planets and all the other bodies surrounding us as
> well as we know the techniques of our craftsmen, so that we can
> use and apply them in the same way for all the purposes for
> which they are suited, thus becoming 'lords and owners' of
> nature. (Liedke 1979, p. 49)

Descartes was looking for a new unshakeable foundation for
philosophy and science, free of religious or ideological prejudices
or arguments from authority. He wanted to find it by using a
method of radical methodological doubt about everything; not
only about the reliability of sensory observations, but also about
the existence of God, other people and the world. When he
applied this doubt, he discovered he could not deny his own
existence as the subject (consciousness) of this doubt. This idea of
his own existence as a thinking subject forced itself on him as a
'clear and distinct idea' which he, with his free ability to make
judgements, had to confirm. Because in his next step he had met a
'clear and distinct' idea of a completely perfect substance, and
because a non-existent perfect substance is impossible, he must
also confirm the existence of God. And because (his third step) it
would be contradictory to its nature for a perfect substance (i.e.
God) continually to deceive human beings in their observations,
we must also confirm the existence of the world and other people.

   This lonely thinking subject, deducing in the end, on the basis
of its own *logos* (*ratio* – thinking), the existence of God, the

world, and other people, then confronts in that world something completely opposite to what it, as consciousness, is: namely, matter, extension.

Here nature will have to be subjected to a particular procedure if it still wants to be nature. It will have to present itself as a geometric quantity. Nature becomes then only that part of its observable expanse which can be measured. This means that, in so far as modern positive sciences still work with this Cartesian understanding of nature, they cannot tell us how nature *is*, but only how nature, under certain circumstances imposed by people, will act. Natural laws discovered during this process are hypotheses whose verification does not depend on nature but on experimental proofs.

Whereas Greek natural science wanted to 'save the phenomena' by looking at them as they present themselves and as they are, showing little interest in technology, the new natural sciences ordered and prepared nature to such a degree that, through investigation, humanity could see what it wants to see. The dualism between humanity and nature which this brings about is more than clear: nature is seen as an extension, while the spirit observing it is without extension.

This also reveals a change in people's attitudes. It began with their stepping back from nature, and came finally to the conclusion that humanity was no longer part of nature. Only its unimportant body still belongs to it (we will discover abundantly what results this has had, especially for the man/woman relationship). Therefore, when humanity interferes in nature (often aggressively), it interferes in something which has become foreign to it, and to which it is not emotionally tied. Humankind is even less inhibited by trepidation before nature, or by respect for nature's intrinsic, individual meaning.

This is one side of the new coin. The other is that nature as it is represented in this modern concept of nature only becomes reality in so far as the thinking person allows it to. Put in a very extreme way: humankind becomes the creator of nature. For this reason humankind can dominate nature at will, use it for its purposes, and be its 'lord and owner' (Liedke 1979, p. 53). The world becomes split into a 'spiritless nature' (*res extensae*) and a 'nature-less spirit' (*res cogitans*).

All inhibitions which would protect or respect nature have

disappeared here. Whether we speak of a subjective theory (only the thinking subject is important) or of an objective praxis (nature viewed as sub-human material), nature as creation has disappeared completely from view (Liedke 1979, pp. 49ff.).

Absolute dualism has thus won its battle; the thinking person has been separated from nature, from everything surrounding it; the thinking spirit is even separated from its own body. In other words, there is an unbridgeable dichotomy between the subject (*res cogitans*) and its object (*res extensae*).

Human existence becomes an 'existence as thinker'. The result of this is that all certainties and experiences derived from sensory perception lose their ability to convince. In one way this rational system of thinking is superior when seen from the object side, because it is universal and can treat everything; everything can become the object of rational empirical research and nothing is unthinkable. Seen in another way, it has its shadow-side when viewed in terms of the thinking subject. This thought system is one-sided and tends to make the subject an absolute, as if it were the only thinkable, truly human way of being.

When humanity is no longer part of nature, of matter, when it, in principle, is separated from it and can only think about it, humanity is cheated of all other types of experience such as music and play, or desire and eros. Above all the subject's own human body becomes a foreign, lifeless object, remaining far behind the rational spirit. Humankind does not live there any more, there is no one at 'home' (cf. Duintjer 1988, pp. 28–34).

3

After providing this explanation, Liedke refers to the results of the chosen starting-point, that is, of nature as extension (*extensio*).
– By concentrating only on those things in nature that can be examined, all other aspects are either excluded or are banned to a marginal position. Environmental interrelationships are an example of one such phenomenon which no longer counted.
– By adopting an ever more specialized approach in research, the larger whole disintegrates, there is no longer anyone with a comprehensive view. The more someone knows about one single element, the more scientific is one's work. This 'particularizing',

which explains everything by dividing it into its smallest parts, has resulted from the *extensio* character of the modern concept of nature.

– By taking into consideration only expanse and measurability, nature's determinism is heavily underlined. No notice is taken of its inner dynamism, its process character. We then see that certain aspects of the medieval image of God are now transferred to nature. The prescience and predetermination with which God is attributed become transformed into a progressive determination of nature. This cannot, it is true, be empirically demonstrated, but that is only the result of a human insufficiency which will sooner or later be mastered.

– Whereas in Greek thinking *time* was the main category, as subject of the event called *physis* (arising, existing, perishing), there is no question of this in modern thinking, where space, the expanse, is the central quantity. Time is now clock time, the distance between the two hands on the clock. This threatens to equate past, present and future and to fixate completely the past and the future.

– Growth in nature could only be understood, according to the modern concept of nature, as quantitative growth. Knowledge in the positive sciences had also, for this reason, a cumulative character. While certain theories disappear in the human sciences because they are replaced by better ones, in the positive sciences knowledge is only increased, nothing disappears. Liedke observes a sort of 'conquer the land' mentality (Liedke 1979, p. 60), which turns positive science and technology into an enterprise, such as the white pioneers' conquest of the American West. As the Native Americans there were exterminated, likewise here nature is 'exterminated'. We must also not neglect to note that the economy offered a stimulus for growth of science and technology which should not be underestimated. The Greek awareness that, in addition to growth, *physis* also included loss was completely disregarded.

– Finally, there is the question of malleability: the extensive, the objective, is open to influence and manipulation. Natural science and technology meet in activity, in experimentation. C. F. von Weizsäcker notes that our sciences' thinking only shows its worth in activity, in a successful experiment (von Weizsäcker 1987). What natural sciences call experience, is an experience in the form of power. It is no wonder that many thinkers in our time are looking for new ways to call a halt to the ecological crisis.

In the context of this book's theme, it has been necessary to point out the shadow side of this one-sided rational philosophy. This does not mean that I want to write off as defective the great systems devised by Descartes and Kant and all the others who followed them. More important than anything else, they have advanced our thinking; and furthermore, they were people of their own time. In our complicated era we have an urgent need to shed light on other aspects of our being human, in order to protect the world, nature, and ourselves from destruction.

'They have advanced our thinking.' Brita Rang again draws our attention to this within the framework of women's studies. Descartes motto, 'I think, therefore I am', has been particularly important for women. A woman is also a *res cogitans*, and is not limited to her body, even though she is often associated with it. Women were challenged and stimulated not only by Descartes' *cogito*, but equally by his *dubio*, his methodological doubt, as a necessary element of thought inherent in the Cartesian system. This led women, in the period after Descartes, to stress the intellectual equality of men and women. They opposed all the traditional attributes and stereotypical qualities which were constantly being foisted upon them. They demanded not only the recognition of their intellectual abilities, but also access to functions in public life. Not only women raised their voices, a number of male authors also agreed (Rang 1989).

4

WOMEN, SLAVES, AND 'SAVAGES'

The revolution described in the previous chapters, a revolution in scholars' thinking and in economic practices, led not only to changes in economic relationships; it also brought about a thorough change in human relationships. For women, this again meant a second-class position in social and cultural life, this time legitimized by their bond with 'nature'. The same fate was shared by the Native Americans and the Blacks who came to the attention of the European peoples in the period of exploratory expeditions and early colonialism. They were considered 'savages', products of 'nature', deprived of all culture.

The anthropological reduction which took place in this way is the subject of this chapter. Many factors play a part in the revolution in thought and action mentioned above. The most important were mentioned in Chapter 3. As yet, one factor of fundamental importance has not been considered here, namely, Aristotle's view. Section 1 is therefore devoted to it. I then look at the consequences of Aristotle's thinking for 'others': for the Indians and Blacks (section 2), for women in general and for the women among these 'others' (section 3). I close with an excursus on hunting, which also has an association with 'the wilderness' (section 4).

1

Aristotle starts his philosophy from reality as he meets it in the world. He is a 'realist'. He also assumes a teleological foundation. This means that all that is has a purpose in itself, which it must realize: 'For *that* which each thing is, when it has come to full development, *that* we call its nature, whether we speak of a man, a house, or a family' (quotation from Aristotle's *Politics* in Lerner 1986, p. 207). This viewpoint leads him to reason backwards from what is, and to accept as given what his society considers normal. It is therefore understandable that for Aristotle the state is a creation of nature. The individual, when isolated, is insufficiently itself. It becomes equally understandable, even evident, that the man who leads the state is by nature a political animal; this in contrast with the woman, who is an apolitical animal, because she plays no role in the state's organization.

This becomes even more clear when we recall that Aristotle sees an analogy between the household and the state. This latter is made up of households. Whoever wants properly to understand the organization of the state, must have insight into the relations within a household. 'The first and smallest elements of the family are master and slave, husband and wife, father and children' (quoted in Lerner 1986, p. 208).

These different relationships are, for Aristotle, dominated by three dichotomies. The first is the 'natural' duality of soul and body. The soul, being spirit, is by nature the ruler over the body, as reason is over the senses and over emotion. Both of these latter are associated with the body.

The second dichotomy is between the free person and the slave. Slavery is therefore for Aristotle a 'natural' necessity. Some are born to rule as free men; others are born to be ruled. Moreover, slaves serve human needs with their body and assume, in so doing, a lower position than the masters who allow themselves to be led by the spirit. Therefore, there is not a great difference between the use made of slaves and that made of tame animals. For this reason Aristotle also calls slaves 'body people'.

Finally, there is the dichotomy between man and woman. This is the most fundamental because it flows not only from the different social positions each assumes. For Aristotle, it is also a strictly biologically based phenomenon. The reasoning from the *de facto* social situation has already been referred to above. It is clarified further when we read how Aristotle describes the different ways in which a free man rules over his slaves, a husband over his wife, and a father over his children. The differences among these depends on the 'nature' of the persons in question: 'The slave has no ability at all to deliberate; the wife has it to a certain degree, but is without authority; the child has it, but is immature. 'From this it follows that their moral virtue is different. Thus Aristotle arrives at the conclusion that a man's courage is displayed in the giving of orders and that of a woman in obeying them (Lerner 1986, p. 208).

As for the biological basis of the dichotomy between man and woman, and the consequent inferiority of the latter to the former, these are revealed in the application of Aristotle's teaching on the four elements to the reproductive process. According to Aristotle, it is possible to distinguish four causes: the *causa materialis*; the *causa efficiens* (which provides the stimulus); the *causa formalis* (which provides the form); and the *causa finalis* (the goal pursued) (Lerner 1986, pp. 205–11). Of these four causes, the material cause is the least important; the word material already says this. In the process of human reproduction, the woman's contribution is limited completely to the terrain of the material cause. The man provides the other three, all of which are of a higher order. His contribution is more spiritual, more divine. The woman contributes only the material (*katamenia*, the menstrual blood) in which the man's seed can grow; she has no role in the composition of the embryo: 'The product of her labour is not hers. The man on the other hand does not labour but works.' The author of this sentence, Maryanne Horowitz, notes correctly here that in this view the product of her exerting work (giving birth) does not belong to the woman herself. The man, on the other hand, does not perform this (slave or paid) labour, but is occupied only with creative, form-giving work (Horowitz, cited in Lerner 1986, p. 207).

In Aeschylus' *Oresteia*, the god Apollo reaches this conclusion when he has to pronounce the final judgement that 'though she is the mother of the child she is not the parent. She takes care of it, and guides the growth of the young seed planted by the true parent, the man' (cited in Lerner 1986, p. 205). To summarize, we can say the following. Aristotle's view of the world is not only dualistic, it is also hierarchical. The soul dominates the body; rational thought, the emotions; people, animals; the masters, their slaves. Each person's 'nature' shows him/her the appropriate place in the hierarchy which he/she is to occupy. We have here one great ascending series of being, which by 'nature' becomes a series of orders (or of acts of obedience). Human society is divided according to the two sexes and according to the differentiation of slave from free. There is the male, who is rational, strong, and gifted with the ability to beget posterity, who is provided with a soul and is fit to rule; and there is the female, who is weak and who only contributes the material to the process of procreation, who is denied a soul and is there to be ruled. In short, just like the slaves, the woman belongs to the 'body' people and to the 'others'. By attributing to slaves a number of the 'naturally' weak female qualities, Aristotle justifies his opinion of the value of slaves, because, just like women, they render service with their bodies.

All this leads to two conclusions:

– Aristotle derives the difference of class in society from the hierarchy of one sex over another. He does this both implicitly and explicitly when he attributes greater value to the work performed by the free, male citizen in public, political life, and to his rational considerations, than to the work done by women at home.

– Aristotle extends his policy on the orderly performance of household duties without interruption to the policy of the state and political life. The state is built and governed on an analogy with the foundation of the patriarchal home in which sexual inequality forms the basis of the dominance over classes and races.

Of course in later years Aristotle's statements were disputed and were corrected by new scientific discoveries. The remarkable aspect is that for centuries even his critics did not argue against the fundamental position as to the inequality of the man/woman relationship, but continued to assume it as a 'natural' given (Lerner 1986, pp. 206–10; Moller Okin 1979, pp. 73–96).

2

I would now like to call attention to the phenomenon belonging to the 'other' in Aristotle's reasoning, to all non-Greeks who were thought to belong to that group. Those who are not free Greek citizens and who do not belong to that nation are *hoi barbaroi*, the barbarians. They too are put in the category of 'body' people, as are slaves and all women.

In the previous chapter we saw, in a way which leaves nothing open to doubt, (1) how the domination over nature was verbalized in terms of claiming the female body; (2) how great were both the fear of nature's unpredictability and explosiveness which disturbed order, and the fear of the irregularities which could turn female sexuality into chaos for the man. To these are added a new category of 'savages', of 'others' who are unknown and who have been assigned in advance a low status: the black slaves and the native Americans. The period between about 1500 and 1700, was when many European countries claimed colonies. They travelled to discover new lands and to remove any treasures from the ground that might be present there.

The early reports of the first explorers still spoke of peaceful and friendly Native Americans – even though they were given a place on the hierarchical ladder somewhere between animals and Europeans. However, soon after, in the early seventeenth century, reports speaking differently became the norm. The Native Americans were said to live as wild animals, without houses or cities, without agriculture or even clothing. They lived there as the first people; they knew no discipline, had no civilization! Native Americans became a symbol of the 'savage' and were more animal-like than the animals which they hunted. They were therefore degraded to 'body' people with uninhibited desires, and they had to be tamed like women and witches. (Merchant 1980, p. 132).

Of course the motives which led the European countries to search for new continents were primarily economic; but the aggressive desire for conquest, possession and exploitation coloured the explorers' attitudes and made painfully clear the total absence of any respect for the nature of the indigenous populations they met. The history of the slave trade – West Africa lost about twenty million people between 1441 and 1860 – and the extermination of the Native Americans on both American continents can only be explained by the fact that white European men did not consider them people but animals. The 'pioneers' put the 'red man' on the same level of civilization as untouched and wild animals. It was even thought that killing Native Americans was a good deed, and this was justified with the idea that their bones first had to fertilize the ground before the white man's plough could rip it open (Liedke 1979, p. 68).

3

While the plundering of the conquered land and the degradation of its inhabitants had its effects on all the indigenous people, for the women among them this treatment had additional results. Until recently they have seldom been mentioned in the literature. Recent work by feminist researchers has shed more light on this hidden side of the 'process of civilization' (Mies 1986, pp. 90ff.). A few examples should suffice.

Rhoda Reddock's investigation of women and slavery in the Caribbean area (cited in Mies 1986, p. 96) demonstrates very clearly that the colonial masters maintained a value system which treated the women among the conquered peoples in a way diametrically opposed to the values they attributed to the women 'at home'. During long periods of their slavery, these women were forbidden to marry or bear children. It was thought less expensive to import slaves than to spend money breeding them. But in the colonists' own society they drove 'their' own women into the homes, to produce more children. These women were cut off from public life and prevented from owning property in their own right.

The aggressive colonization of new continents was legitimized as a mission brought by Christian civilization to the local inhabitants. Two trends come together in this period: the suppression and punishment of impoverished European women in a massive witch hunt, and the suppression (under the guise of 'civilization') and punishment of 'barbarian' peoples in the colonies. Both categories were unrestrained, dangerous, and just as much a part of savage 'nature'; both were subjected to superior strength and brute force to break their resistance to this expropriation and exploitation.

A second example involves the behaviour of colonists in Burma. Maria Mies quotes from a book by Fielding Hall entitled *A People at School*. Hall was a political officer of the British colonial administration in Burma between 1887 and 1891. In his book he gives a lively report of the independence of Burmese women, of the equality between the sexes he observes there, and of the peaceful character of the population, which he attributes to Buddhism. But Hall fears that these factors will not raise a profit for the colonial masters. He draws the conclusion that Burma has to be put on the road to progress, but, of course, according to *his* ideas and norms: 'We rule over our own subjects and we do so in our own way. Our presence here conflicts totally with their own desires.' For this Briton, equality between the sexes is a sign of underdevelopment. For this reason, the British colonialists have to destroy the independence of these women, and they have to teach the men the 'virtues' of sexism and militarism. He offers the following advice on measures to be taken 'to civilize' the Burmese people. In the first place, the men must be taught to fight and kill for their British masters: 'I cannot suggest anything better for these people than that they should have their own regiment in which to distinguish themselves in our wars. This should open their eyes to new views on life' (cited by Mies 1986, p. 93). His further advice is that the women must give up their freedom for the benefit of the men.

Speaking of the equality between the sexes which he had observed as signs of backwardness, Fielding Hall warns, 'We must not forget that their civilization is about a thousand years behind our own.' And he adds to this:

> What the surgeon's knife is to the sick bed, is the soldier's sword to sick nature. The gospel of progress, of knowledge, of happiness ... is not taught in books and sermons but by the spear and the sword. Can there be anything worse than to declare, as does Buddhism, that bravery is of no importance and than to say to the men, as their women have done, that they are no better and no more than they [the women]? (cited in Mies 1986, p. 93)

Fielding Hall appeals here to an opinion, held by the ethnologists of his time, that young civilizations show little or no difference between men and women (no gender differences); 'higher' civilization, on the other hand, is characterized by a distinct difference between the two, which in practice comes down to the woman's inequality. Risseeuw speaks of the 'gender' transformation which the British in their colonial period also applied to women in Sri Lanka. On the one hand, the British feeling of superiority and the resulting duty to 'raise' up 'inferior' peoples played a role; on the other hand, economic interests were an important incentive (Risseeuw 1988, pp. 407–8).

Meanwhile, there is no doubt that people have always been very ambivalent in their view of nature, in the sense of the untouched, 'savage' wilderness and the people who lived there, the 'savages'. It depended on which situation and from which position it was examined. When economic interests were involved, the 'savages' no longer counted as people. They became objects to be traded or denigrated. Women and men, each in their own 'suitable' manner, were treated as disenfranchised infants.

But on occasions other desires and feelings can be noted among Western men, as in the period of Romanticism, when there was a tendency for the urban technological man to romanticize the 'savage' and to see in him the 'noble savage'. Because of their unfamiliarity, these people became idealized, and the wilderness became an escape, a chance to step out of everyday Western reality.

The cultural philosopher Ton Lemaire tells us that the 'savages' have never really been observed by Western people in their own reality, and that the meaning of their culture has never been examined for its intrinsic value. Either they are degraded as instruments to benefit our urge to conquer, or else they are idealized, but that also happens for our benefit (Lemaire 1985, pp. 24–28). This observation profoundly moved me, for it parallels the way women are looked upon by and from Western culture. Women are always evaluated from an androcentric point of view: be it as inferior, as a mere body with emotions and passions, or as an instrument for procreation and for the care of daily household life; or be it as exalted, as Muse, as guardian angel, as the Virgin Mary, pure and chaste, as 'The Lady', as the poetry in the daily prose, and thus also as a means of escape.

Whereas women were first characterized by more animal and corporeal characteristics which men rejected but which secretly fascinated them, in the eighteenth and nineteenth centuries we note a change. She is now looked upon as mistress of the home and family and is released from her sexuality. 'Woman is a glass cover over an empty space.' This comment by the author Lema Holm (cited in Van den Berg 1957, p. 159) is a distressing witness to female sexuality taken over by a patriarchal culture and alienated from women. It is now expected from the woman that, with a gentle hand and tender glance, she guide along the right path the hot-headed male who must daily fight his way in the hostile world. However, this change only affected women in the middle and aristocratic classes, since it was still customary to look down upon women from the working class who had to toil at hard labour in factories and elsewhere.

One last association with 'wilderness', namely hunting, has also been borrowed from Lemaire. The starting-point is a 1959 essay written by the famous Spanish philosopher Ortega y Gasset, entitled 'The Happiness of the Hunt' (cited in Lemaire 1985, pp. 31–5). He introduces the notion that in our society hunting is the artificial restoration of a primitive, archaic situation in which humanity once again hurls itself completely into the untouched wilderness. Hunting becomes a return to the wilderness outside ourselves, and at the same time a return to the 'natural person' within. For Gasset, this submersion in nature is a healing regeneration and a revitalization of his own forces, abilities and passions. It is in fact a luxurious form of cultural criticism, an interruption of normal life in order to return to it later with renewed vitality.

While Ortega y Gasset compares this situation of the hunter with that of the philosopher, who as a hunter in the field of ideas wanders about and exercises his alertness, Lemaire is more realistic in seeing in the hunt a symbol of the position of the upper classes. Hunting has for centuries been a privilege of the nobility, and later of the financially well off. It is also an almost exclusively male pursuit. Hunting conjures up associations of power, conquest and battle, but is also a symbol of the typically male attitude and role in eroticism and sexuality. Penetrating the forest, becoming master of the (wild) animals, the pursuit and killing of animals was not only a tense adventure, but it also elicited feelings of lust, of power and of superiority (Lemaire 1985, pp. 31–3).

The comparison is unavoidable where women are the 'prey'. Often I have heard young girls and women sigh, 'Hunting season is open!' The desire to conquer, to be the better of a rival, to 'possess' a woman, even if only physically, with consent or without, are symptoms of it. . . . The more difficult the conquest, the more exciting the hunt! It is even thought that women like this: they fight, they resist, and in this way show they are pleased to be 'taken'. These are approximately the same words which Bacon and others use to express themselves when they discuss the conquest and domination of Mother Nature.

As Tennyson observed, 'The man is the hunter, the woman his prey'.

5

KNOWING NATURE

In this chapter the erotic sexual metaphors we find in the language of philosophers and scientists take centre stage. In treating this aspect of the question I rely primarily on the book by Evelyn Fox Keller entitled *Reflections on Gender and Science*.

First, an introduction is necessary to explain exactly what this theme involves (section 1). Next, Plato's epistemology is used as a first example (section 2), Bacon's as a second (section 3); an example of hermetic, alchemist thinking is used as a third (section 4). A review of the consequences for women and for nature follows as a conclusion (section 5).

1

Even the title of Evelyn Fox Keller's book *Reflections on Gender and Science* requires a certain amount of explanation. In feminist studies and theory formation it has become necessary to make a distinction between sex and gender. 'Sex' has to do with the type of body we are given at birth; we are born as woman or man. 'Gender' includes more than this; it is the cultural definition of the behaviour that in a given society and at a particular moment of its history is assigned to the one sex or the other. Gender means a social or cultural set of roles and attitudes attributed to a given sex. Sex therefore has a biological meaning; gender, in its turn, has a cultural meaning (Lerner 1986, p. 238).

In feminist discussions, the two concepts need to be kept strictly separated from one another. As Gayle Rubin has observed, every society recognizes the system in which 'the biological natural resources of human sexuality and procreation are shaped by human intervention and by society, a system in which the needs in this area are satisfied in a conventional way, however bizarre some of these conventions may be' (cited in Outshoorn 1989, p. 14).

Now, to turn back to Fox Keller. In her book she submits deeply rooted superstition to criticism, examining whether its objectivity, reasoning, and spirit are 'male' and its subjectivity, feeling and nature are 'female'. In this separation of emotional and intellectual labour, women guarantee and protect the personal, the emotional and the particular, while science, as the domain of the impersonal, the rational and the general, is reserved for the male sphere. The result of this division is twofold:
– the exclusion (until recently still generally valid) of women from scientific occupations is symptomatic;
– but more important is the deeper chasm arising between the male and the female, the subjective and the objective, even between love and power; a division in the structure of humanity which is sanctioned by an objectivist concept of science.

Fox Keller describes the mechanism of this dichotomy by using the important stages of the Western history of science as examples: Plato's philosophy; the alchemy of the middle ages; the modern empirical investigation of nature; the quantum theory; and, finally, modern biological engineering. She then shows that present-day feminist criticism and theory of science can be brought together in a shared attempt to eliminate this division.

The question which Fox Keller now puts is: To what degree is the nature of science inseparable from the image of maleness, and what would it mean for science if things were different? What she is really asking is, therefore: How has the way of looking at man and woman (gender) influenced the construction of the sciences? Women, men and the sciences are together the product of a complicated, dynamic process, in which cognitive emotional and social forces are woven together.

Fox Keller refers to a work by T. S. Kuhn entitled *The Structure of Scientific Revolutions* (1962), which treats the changes in the social and political context of scientific development, and the creation of new paradigms in science as a result of these changes. Kuhn argues that it normally takes a long time not only to develop these new paradigms, to accept them and to apply them, but also to become able to draw genuinely decisive consequences from them.

His book calls in question the opinion, until then generally accepted, that science is autonomous and absolutely progressive, and that it is moving step by step in the direction of a correct description of reality 'as it is'.

Although the majority of scientists have recognized in the mean time that science is also the expression of certain desires and that it is influenced by factors such as political and social pressures, they have not drawn any consequences from this knowledge for the production of scientific theories. Most of them still think that 'natural laws are as impersonal and free of value judgments as are the rules of mathematics. We did not want it that way, but that is the way it is' (Fox Keller 1985, pp. 7–10).

Research in the area of women's studies wants not only to discover and explain the roots of the diverse dichotomies in general use (such as those between the personal and the political; between subjectivity and objectivity; between feeling and reason), and in this way to take seriously the situation of women, but it also wants to include the areas of human experience which were assigned to women, namely, the personal, the emotional and the sexual. Precisely when it concerns science, this latter also implies giving attention to the personal, emotional and sexual dimensions of male experience. This brings Fox Keller to the results of research in the positive sciences and the present criticism of these results. She notes that our natural laws are more than merely an expression of objective research results, and more even than the results of political and social pressure: they must also be tested for their personal and traditionally male content. And it then appears that a reference to reality as 'natural laws which are impersonal and free of all human value judgments' is characteristic of the 'impersonal, anonymous and objective' (Fox Keller, 1985, p. 15).

After this introduction, I reach the theme of this chapter: the names used for nature and the use of metaphors in this area. Assigning names to nature is one of science's main tasks. Theories, models and descriptions are such names worked out in more detail. We now reach the question: How do we arrive at knowledge; how can we acquire it? The answer to this has to do with the representation of spirit and nature, of subject and object, which lies at its basis.

In Western history, one of the most frequently used metaphors for such a relationship is that of sexual relations. This is already to be found in the Bible. To know is a form of relationship, just as sex is a form of knowledge. Both are driven forward by a sort of desire. Even though the experience of knowing is rooted in the physical, the corporeal, it does not remain there. It is typical of knowledge that it tries to escape from the physical, to transcend the corporeal. The spirit is not simply immanent in the material, it also transcends it. This means that all representations of knowledge are confronted with the dialectics of transcendence and immanence. In this confrontation there is often mention of a wrestling between all that is associated with sex and all that is associated with gender. To be well aware of how variable its meaning has appeared to be over the ages is very much to the point.

Fox Keller identifies three examples which demonstrate the history of these changes. In all three, sexual involvement is present, but the gender associations are different and therefore so too are the metaphors which are used for this knowledge relationship between the knower and the known.

2

The first example is Plato's theory of knowledge (Fox Keller 1985, pp. 25ff.). He is the first philosopher in Western thinking who explicitly and systematically made use of the language of sexuality to reveal his theories of knowledge. What Plato has in common with his predecessors is that he accepts a connection between spirit and nature: *logos*, rationality, is present in both; the spirit is connected with nature and nature is permeated with the spirit. But nature has ambiguous elements: it is not held together completely by the *logos*, but remains imprisoned in an essential dualism. On the one hand it is receptive to the light of reason and order, on the other hand it is equally susceptible to the mysterious powers of irrationality and disorder. What Plato has done is to develop a theory of knowledge which was invulnerable to the undermining forces of the irrational and which gave the spirit the ability to reach transcendence, even though it remains in a state of tension with the immanent. His radical starting-point is that the real object of knowledge must be defined as something which is totally outside the grasp of temporal, material nature. For Plato, truth can only be reached in the realm of pure and absolute Being. A person can reach this, because it is possible to learn to look through the realm of the purely corporeal and come out above it. Only through the purification in which nature is as it were made immaterial and the spirit incorporeal, can a true unification of spirit and nature take place.

In Plato's theory of knowledge, variable matter is left behind and is relinquished to the forces of the irrational, the coincidental and the chaotic. But then we are left with the question: How can the spirit which is anchored in a mortal body find its way to the truth in spite of this? We find the surprising answer in his *Symposium*: the spirit discovers knowledge when it is led by Eros! Just as desire brings forth love, so does love bring forth knowledge.

However, the problem is that Eros propels in two different directions: on the one hand towards reason and on the other towards passion. The dialectic of transcendence and immanence is now depicted in the realm of Eros. Plato's dilemma can be characterized as a struggle between unity and variety. The image of Eros is a good reflection of the fundamental problem of knowledge: How can variety be dissolved in unity; how can subject be matched with object, and 'becoming' be transformed into 'being'?

Throughout Plato's work two fundamental divisions are always observable: the difference between logical and physical nature; and, connected with it, the difference between homosexual and heterosexual Eros (Fox Keller 1985, p. 28).

For Plato, heterosexual desire has nothing to do with transcendence, especially because it is associated with corporeal reproduction. Children are the result of animal urges, but knowledge is the result of a divine coming together of related substances. It is the experiences of a man's loving a boy, not a woman, which had formed the first impetus for Plato's philosophy and his theory of knowledge. Here there is a question of like uniting with like; from this it follows that Eros, which is important because it is a step towards the realm of the Being of Ideas, is homoerotic. (In Plato's world, the joining of a man with a woman was not an image of the coming together of like with like!) In order to avoid endangering the separation between transcendence and immanence, it is necessary that this homosexuality should not regress into purely corporeal desire and satisfaction. In sexuality, just as in knowledge, the tension between unity and variety brings about a harmony which continually becomes more complex in that it refers back to the tension-filled relationship between love and aggression, equality and hierarchy, co-operation and dominance.

Thus for Plato the only relevant erotic model was that of the joining of an adult man (who loves) and a young man (who is loved) of a similar social position. Decisive for the legitimacy of this paedophile relation is that each retains his own value; that neither becomes submissive to the other; that, although sensual desire be experienced, every sexual satisfaction is denied, so that this relationship transforms physical excitement into imaginative and intellectual energy. Therefore, what we have here, though not totally, is a rather emancipated erotic relationship in which desire and control go hand in hand. Passion had to be mastered, but not love.

Finally, for Plato, Eros is directed towards the spiritual, the elevating. The older man can, indeed, receive impressions of beauty through the handsome young man, but their joining is rather an exercise and a means to reach the contemplation of the eternal Ideas which surpass all sensual pleasure.

In this way Plato developed a model of homoerotic love which allows a mutual experience of desire, without being disrespect of the masculinity or dignity of the beloved, without creating a subdivision into dominating and subordinate roles, or causing the aggression which such a situation implies. But a price has to be paid for this harmony, and this is sexual control, which is a necessity if the goal of knowledge and of absolute beauty is to be reached. If this control does not work, the irrational and the aggressive threaten to return, and the partners will be unable to attain the goal, that is, knowledge and absolute beauty. In this theory of knowledge, it comes down to a separation of order from chaos, of Eros from aggression, of the spirit from the sensual body. Within the given model, a place *is* provided for a certain degree of hierarchy (the elder, the lover, leads; the youth follows), but not for dominance. It provides a metaphor for a kind of knowledge which is erotic but which continues to suffer from its own inner contradictions. Just as in the metaphor where, in the end, we are less concerned with the beloved than with the 'image' of the Idea in him, so it is that there is not so much interest in knowing the concrete objects in themselves, as in knowing the Forms to which they refer. Plato's whole philosophical system, as it is outlined in his theory of love, is permeated with indifference towards the body, the individual as such. Concentration on the Idea always leads away from the personal and the typical. Because Plato excludes matter from his theory of knowledge and from his definition of the ideal Eros, the perfected sexuality, he is not able to include genuine equality in his observations. His ideal of knowledge is viewing Being, the Beautiful, and not conquering and possessing all that is knowable (Fox Keller 1985, pp. 25–35).

3

Although the modern scientist borrows the dividing line between the logical and the physical from Plato, and also maintains it in the division of theoretical from experimental research, and of pure from applied science, it is the physical world which is put foremost in scientific considerations. In so doing the scientist inevitably pushes aside Plato's objection to recognizing the material world and ends up with the aggression which Plato wanted to avoid. Modern natural sciences no longer study the Platonic Forms, that elevated distillation of male sexuality, but material nature, the physical framework of female sexuality. It is therefore an obvious choice that Fox Keller takes the figure of Francis Bacon as her second example of the change in sexual metaphors for knowledge and science, Bacon, who lived two thousand years after Plato and who is the herald of the new science.

Although I have already discussed Bacon's significance in an earlier chapter, I would like to make a few additional comments in the context of this chapter, and in so doing also clarify the meaning of his metaphors. Bacon becomes thus the *second* example of the imagery used of the relationship between the knower and the known (Fox Keller 1985, pp. 38ff.).

Contrary to Plato, Francis Bacon is no longer the natural scientist who sees cohesion as the goal of knowledge; for him it is power, and with it the domination of nature. The image of the homoerotic union is replaced by that of heterosexual conquest and by a process of subjugation. Bacon does not look upon science as an elevated love relationship to the 'essential nature of things', but as a 'chaste and legal marriage between spirit and nature'.

The purity of this marriage provides the boundaries between the two and guarantees, within this delimitation, the differences between the two consorts: nature is, of course, subject to laws, but itself has no spirit. This purity fulfils in Bacon's metaphor a comparable function to that of the sexual repression which in Plato's metaphor provides the separation between Eros and aggression. But now the accents lie elsewhere: purity for Bacon protects the knower and the object known, not against aggression but against Eros. In neither of the two theories is material nature (which for both Plato and Bacon is female) included in a partner-like relationship; in the first it is referred to a lower level and in the second it is seduced and subjugated. In all the differences between Plato and Bacon, it is striking to note the degree to which the changes are the direct result of Plato's own division between the spiritual and the physical, between the erotic and the aggressive. The hierarchical relationship between spirit and matter, between male and female, which Bacon borrows from Plato's view of the world, includes the aggression which Plato wanted to avoid.

We have already discussed earlier how Bacon's imagery is permeated with sexual metaphors which colour the penetration and conquest of nature by science. Fox Keller points out a further complication: it is not so much science's goal to do violence to nature 'against her will', but to dominate it 'by following the dictates of the truly natural'. This implies that it is 'natural' to lead nature, to shape it and to subjugate it, because only in this way can the true 'nature of things' be revealed. For this reason, science has to exercise control and domination, since these dictates include a desire to be dominated. This would mean that nature has asked to be conquered with superior force and aggression! Or, to use another image: nature plays 'hide and seek' like an innocent child, in the hope it will be found (Farrington 1964, p. 92). There is even discussion here of 'divine nature'; but we note that in that case the 'she' is then changed to 'he'.

The title of Bacon's early work *The Male Birth of Time* leaves no doubt as to the author's intent: up until then male science has only produced female children who were passive, weak and hesitant. But now a son has been born who is active, forceful and able to beget life. For this it was necessary that the spirit, in order to become truly masculine and virile, be purged of all misleading prejudices so that it can observe without hindrance. By first admitting his insufficiency as incompetent spirit, and opening himself to perfection by God, he must then pass along a 'female' path before he can become a potent, virile mediator in the relationship with nature. If this transformation succeeds, he can then in his turn speak to 'his son' and pass on to him his method of knowledge and science, which he himself begot.

4

And finally I come to the *third* example of still another metaphor which reflects the relation between knower and known. This comes from the more organically orientated hermetic philosophy, and from the thinking arising from magical and alchemist directions. However different these too may be in their concrete opinions, they have two characteristics in common: a great respect for the cosmos and for nature, as well as the conviction that all things that live, move and grow in nature are based on the co-operation of two principles, namely, the male and the female. The sexual metaphor used, which is what we are concerned with here, is coitus, the joining and melting together of the male and the female principles in order to reach knowledge (Fox Keller 1985, p. 54).

These alchemist and hermetic trends existed long before the transition to the modern time through Bacon and others reached its conclusion. But even then they continued working in their opposition to the purely empirical approach to nature. In the seventeenth century, therefore, we see, especially in England, that there is a bitter struggle between two mutually exclusive camps in science and in philosophy, namely, between the hermetic and the mechanistic thought patterns. In the hermetic tradition nature was permeated with a divine spirit. In order to understand this it was necessary for heart, hands and reason to work together and to influence one another. The mechanistic philosophy, in contrast with this, wanted to separate matter from the spirit, and the hands (experiments!) from reason and the heart.

The hermetic literature, collected together in the *Corpus Hermeticum* from the first three centuries after Christ and named after Hermes Trismegistos, is made up of two types of writings:

the 'popular', about astrology and the occult, and the 'scholarly' in the areas of philosophy and theology. The idea behind the popular works is that the cosmos has been composed as a unity and that all of its parts are dependent on one another. In order to understand how this works it is necessary to know the laws of sympathy and antipathy which keep the various parts of the universe bound together. Science was unable to prove this, and thus it was attributed to divine revelation.

Even in that early period there was a growing distrust of the traditional Greek rationalism (as found in Aristotle). A more profound bond between science and religion was offered as an alternative to rationalism. The theological writings which arose in this context are characterized by an honest piety of the mystical type.

The Arabs also practised Hermeticism, and through them it also had its influence on Albert the Great, on the alchemists, and also on Paracelsus (sixteenth century), among others. In particular the alchemists from the seventeenth century were strongly influenced by the works of Paracelsus, a Swiss doctor and alchemist. His thought is based primarily on a visionary neo-Platonic philosophy in which the life of an individual is believed to be inseparable from that of the universe. The alchemists in the seventeenth century had a universal science in mind which would be able to explain the whole world given by nature. Their success and their influence is to be found mainly in the areas of chemistry and the production of pharmaceutical products. They opposed, above all, a dogmatic and rational philosophy and theology, and the rigidity of the universities. When the language and the imagery which both they and Bacon used are examined, the differences are striking and interesting. Bacon thought in terms of a 'chaste and legal marriage between spirit and nature' that would put nature in the service of humanity, that would make it a slave, and in this way emphasized the separation between the two and the domination of the one by the other. The alchemists had a completely different metaphor in mind, that of coitus, the coming together of spirit and nature, the flowing together of the male and the female. Bacon's metaphor was that of the virile super-man; that of the alchemists was the hermaphrodite. Their metaphor expressed the cohesion and the co-operation of the male and the female elements.

When the alchemists speak in their texts about 'marriage', they refer to the principle of harmony, such as that which lies at the basis of the relationship of the sun and the moon. They believed in an inner affinity of the whole world which was a living creation, always built up of the 'male and the female', and in which the parts are united just because of their reciprocal love (Merchant 1980, p. 49).

Thus the alchemists believed in the necessity of the bond between the male and the female, and based this on the principles of symmetry and of equality. They are the rightful heirs of Paracelsus, who saw in the sun and the moon two equal elements, male and female, king and queen.

One of this view's most fervent proponents, Thomas Vaughan, has written:

> For life is nothing else than a unity of the male and the female principles, and he who knows this secret perfectly is also familiar with the secrets of marriage – both spiritual and natural – ... Marriage is not a plain, trivial matter, but has a sacramental dimension. It is a visible sign of our invisible unity with Christ. (cited in Fox Keller 1985, p. 50)

Now, we must not think that with these images there was any serious belief in the equality of men and women as *people*; what we have here are rather images which relate to the organic nature, but which despite this are, historically, very interesting.

Although both contradictory directions encourage science, both in research and in experiment, we hear from the hermetical camp the advice: 'I would like to encourage you to listen to the magical power in the Magician's saying, listen with the reason of the heart!' This quotation from Vaughan agrees with what his teacher Paracelsus had written a century earlier: 'The art of the "Doctor" has its roots in the heart'; and also: 'the healing power of medicines is discovered in true love' (cited in Fox Keller 1985, p. 60).

Joseph Glanvill, a representative of the Royal Society, a newly-established association of natural scientists, disputed these opinions. He warned against the power which our affections have over our so easily seduced reason: 'The woman in us still sticks to us.' Glanvill reaches the conclusion that truth does not have a chance when 'the affections are wearing the pants and when the female rules' (cited in Fox Keller 1985, p. 58).

Thus science must be male; and then, let it be understood, without heart, without tenderness, without love, without Eros. The goal of the new science as defended by the Royal Society is not metaphysical interaction, but power; not the unity of spirit and matter, but the establishment of a world dominance of humanity over nature. If the 'alternative' hermetic tendency had a strong social involvement, both in the direction of health care as well as that of the many groups which struggled for independence (such as the sects), the members of the Royal Society showed rather a penchant for retreating into their scientific ivory towers.

5

Here too, at the end of this chapter, we can ask ourselves again the question: What were the results of all this for women and for nature? In the first place, this whole state of affairs meant the defeat of the way of thinking in which women and nature were seen as 'holy' or as 'divine', but it also meant the defeat of a science which would have guaranteed to both of these at least a vestige of respect. Furthermore, it will become clear that the two tendencies mentioned above became mixed up in the emotional discussions about the knowledge which women had of nature, of herbs, and thus of medicine, and they let their voice be heard. It was one of contempt and hate on the one hand and one of a certain degree of understanding and good-will on the other.

Finally, I would like once more to focus attention on how very much the radical changes which took place during the seventeenth century affected the concepts of role as applied to the two sexes.

We have to look at the connection which still exists between the social, economic and political changes against the background of these important scientific changes. Namely, the changes in the image of woman and in the concept of nature have been strongly determined by the new science and in this way have been put in the spotlight. A strict polarization comes into existence between the roles dictated to men and especially those dictated to women. All was ruled by a kind of fear of exceeding limits in this area (also in clothing), a fear of women who were 'male' in their 'gender' and of men who acted 'female'. Women were made insignificant and the power of men was increased.

Of course the scientific revolution did not bring about these changes, but it supported them in that it legitimized the polarization in the meaning attributed to the two sexes, which symbolized the separation of the spirit from nature, of reason from emotion, of the objective from the subjective. A lifeless, mechanized view of nature went together with the denial of the woman's sexuality. The new science demanded rationality and objectivity from the man, as well as the will to dominate nature. We see that it becomes a characteristic of modern science that it defines itself in opposition to all that is 'female'. In this way fears are banished, the principle of the 'maternal' (cf. Latin *mater* and mater-ial) is tamed, and the man's strength is confirmed. It is true that the more 'alternative' voices in philosophy and science were not silenced, but they had lost their case, and no longer had the power to contradict the ideology with regard to the sexes, let alone to stop it (Fox Keller 1985, pp. 61–5).

6

WOMAN'S 'NATURE'

We have given a good deal of attention to the radical changes which were begun in the sixteenth century and which were put into practice in the seventeenth century in the thinking, the observations and the behaviour of the leading philosophers and scientists, and which had important consequences for society. In this chapter I would like to take this argument one step further, and say something about the discussions which continued in the eighteenth century on the opposition of nature and culture and the evaluation it implies for men and women. There have been many such discussions, and they have often contradicted one another. In England they followed a different course than in France, each time according to the differing political, social and economic situations which gave rise to them.

In this chapter I would like to highlight the thought and writings of the influential French philosopher Jean Jacques Rousseau. In his works the themes 'nature' and 'woman' are treated in detail (section 1). From this discussion on woman and nature it seems we need to take only a small step to reach the 'nature *of* woman'. It is on just this subject that Rousseau, as well as many other thinkers and writers of the eighteenth and nine-teenth centuries, has spoken both uninhibitedly and extensively (section 2).

1

The Franco-Swiss philosopher and moralist Jean Jacques Rousseau lived from 1712 to 1778. He has remained in the collective memory of all levels of the population for coining the motto, 'Back to nature!' But Rousseau cannot be so easily labelled and dismissed.

It is striking that during this period, the Enlightenment, nature in general receives a higher status than before, when it was still associated with the 'savages', with a lack of education, and with original sin. The authors from whom I take the following information are Maurice Bloch and Jean H. Bloch (Bloch and Bloch 1980). On a global scale they distinguish four fields of meaning which have been attributed to 'nature' during the Enlightenment.

1. Nature was seen as referring to a period which chronologically precedes the ordered political state. It is a 'natural condition' in which people live in family units each of which is independent of the others. This 'natural condition' has not yet been infected by the false knowledge and the corruption which are the products, the fruits, of a society based on a social contract. In fact, Rousseau sees the 'natural condition' not so much as a historical reality to which he wishes to return; for him it is rather an abstraction which he applies as a norm in order to reach a better state with a better social contract and in which the 'natural condition' is harmoniously integrated.

2. A second area giving meaning to nature, as we meet it in Rousseau, has to do with humanity as a natural being, with the value of the internal processes of the human body, especially the instincts, emotions and senses, but also the processes of reproduction. Rousseau has the opinion that the better our senses are trained, the better will be our ideas. Other thinkers reach the opposite conclusion. But there is a general agreement on the basic idea that they recognize the results of what the senses can learn from nature.

3. A third possibility is that nature refers to the universal order which implies the harmonious coexistence of human nature and the external world of plants, animals and landscape. In Rousseau's work *Emile*, nature is given its most elevated role. In this work he describes how education must bring about a perfect harmony between art and nature, taking into consideration nature's intentions. Nature here plays the role of guide. The young man Emile has to be brought up to adulthood without the cultural prejudices and contamination which would distract him from his 'nature'.

4. Finally, Rousseau gives 'nature' the meaning of something erotic; and it is used in this way to qualify the lifestyle of the primitive peoples, whether this is real or whether it lives in the imagination, or whether it is a mixture of the two. In this romantic view we are not concerned with 'savages' in a negative

sense, but rather just the opposite. Rousseau saw 'primitive' peoples and also farmers as less corrupt and more natural than society in the cities and at court. He himself, and Diderot especially, saw in these primitives the examples of the virtues of a natural society.

Among all the differences which there indeed are, there is a common conclusion, that nature may no longer be despised and is no longer inferior. On the contrary, it is the source of a new purity and a new vitality (Bloch and Bloch 1980, p. 31).

We see again that the concept 'nature' is ambiguous and layered and is always used in contrast with something else. In this case, for Rousseau and others, it is seen in contrast with society in general, and especially society in France; with the arts and sciences; with the culture (of the upper class), and with civilization. Basically, nature appears to be a category offering a challenge rather than being a clear element in a stable oppositional contrast. This is very clearly expressed when the different philosophies give their opinion of 'nature and woman', of 'women and nature', which sometimes leads to their opinions on 'the feminine nature'.

It is striking that many philosophers, whether they wrote in England or Germany, and particularly Rousseau, amid all their radical urges to reform, remained very hesitant as soon as the discussion turned to women and *their* social and political position. However well spoken Rousseau's pleadings for the 'natural' may have been, his analyses of what was natural for 'the man' and for women were very different. He maintains his hold on the tradition, begun with Aristotle and even earlier, where a woman's nature is defined in terms of her sexual and reproductive functions and goals in life, whereas he writes about the man in terms of a general unlimited potential of rational thought and creativity.

However radical Rousseau's thought was on a number of subjects, and however paradoxical his utterances could be for his contemporaries, what he had to say about women (which originally in earlier works did leave room for the equality of women and men) reveals an orthodox and even conservative point of view. His starting-point appears to give hope. Rousseau begins with the position that men and women are clearly and unmistakably the same in all that is not associated with sexual differences. Thus, everything which they have in common relates to the species; and everything which separates them relates to sex. But then he comes out with the presupposition that it can be proved that the physiological differences between man and woman exert influence on their *moral* being. Precisely this latter now becomes a central theme and colours all possible discussions on the superiority of one sex to the other, and with this all discussion of their possible equality. Nature has made the two sexes different, but each perfect in its own way. They are clearly intended to complement one another, and they cannot be compared with one another in matters which they do not have in common, thus Rousseau.

Just as Rousseau's judgement on nature seems ambiguous, likewise his view of woman, and the man/woman relation, is inconsistent. The initial equality from which he proceeds must quickly clear the field for the conviction that man and woman are 'equal but different'. This motto, in all the centuries following Rousseau's, has played an important role; for just this 'different', this being other, has left more than enough place to apply the familiar gender constructions. On the basis of the biological differences, the thesis of complementarity is preserved. The dominant, androcentric culture fills in the 'poles' with the characteristics it chooses, and the result appears not seldom to be that women are considered supplementary to men (cf. Halkes 1984, ch. 5).

This starting-point provides Rousseau with a biological basis for his analysis which suggests the idea that the man is necessarily strong and active and the woman necessarily weak and passive. This is the reason why the woman is made to please the man. But should the man also feel the need to please, then he does so from his position of strength. For Rousseau this is the law of nature. And further, he claims that because a woman's power to arouse a man's desire is always greater than can be fulfilled, she is, in fact, in a stronger position for negotiating, and so, by using this 'natural' hold over the man, she can influence his moral regeneration by inspiring him to virtuous and heroic deeds. This is even more true when she is providing the same service for the next generation, but then only when she gives expression to her natural condition in an appropriate way, which is, according to Rousseau, motherhood. He is also convinced that returning to the practice of maternal breast-feeding would in itself bring about a total reformation. Even Rousseau's much beloved and often repeated proposition, that of humanity's natural goodness (innocence), becomes endangered when he thinks about woman: 'it is only just that this sex shares our afflictions/evils (*la peine des maux*) whose cause she herself is' (cited in Bloch and Bloch 1980, p. 35).

These different ways of looking at man and woman come together in an intriguing way in Rousseau's book *Emile*, a treatise on education. In it Rousseau explains his ideas in detail. He starts with those about the young man, Emile. If he wants to continue following a virtuous path in his growth to adulthood, then he must avoid the corrupt society of his time and preserve his natural goodness. But once he has become an adult he needs a suitable (female) companion, whom the author introduces as Sophie. The presupposition seems obvious to us, that if Sophie wants to be considered suitable to share her life with Emile, she will have to undergo a similar education. But this is by no means the case.

For Emile nature was the necessary authority which would enable him to become a free man; but for Sophie, nature is already present *in* her, and this becomes the reason for her subjugation. While Emile's education in nature is intended to put all emphasis on his freedom and independence, that of Sophie was there only to accent her dependence and limitation in order to prepare her for her future natural dependence on her husband which will last for the rest of her life.

We can now distinguish two lines in Rousseau's argument (Bloch and Bloch 1980, pp. 30–40). On the one hand, he believes that society makes humanity less natural, robs it of its naturalness. Nevertheless, he can imagine a new individual (a man?) who would be able to unify the demands both of nature and of society in his life.

On the other hand, he insists that Sophie, from within the unnatural order called society, must remain close to nature. For the mother is Nature itself and the woman must not turn away from it. Emile is advised to give no attention to public opinion, yet Sophie is warned to beware of the judgement of this opinion! Emile has to develop all the possibilities his life offers and so continue to grow, but for Sophie this is not necessary; she only has to remain faithful to her 'essence'. According to Rousseau, women remain as children, which he deduced from the fact that their voices do not change at puberty . . .

One quotation can provide a good summary of all this: Men
and women are made for one another, but their mutual
dependence is not of the same nature: men are dependent on
women because of their desires and urges; women are dependent on men both because of their urges and because of their
needs; we could survive better without them than they without
us. In order for them to have all they need for their place in life,
we have to give it to them, we have to want to give it to them,
we have to consider them worth the effort; they are dependent
on our feelings, on the price which we think they are worth and
on the measure to which we respect their charms and virtues.
According to the law of nature itself, women, as far as they
themselves are concerned and their children as well, are
entirely at the mercy of the graciousness and judgment of men.
(cited by Moller Okin 1979, p. 119)

I am therefore in total agreement with Maurice and Jean Bloch,
that from the work of the French Enlightenment philosophers (in
our case Rousseau) we can develop a good insight into the
mechanics and development of the ideology surrounding the two
sexes. They note that 'dormant' fragments of an ideology can
again come into effect and can undermine new ideas, such as
those arising in the Enlightenment. According to the Blochs, it
appears as if the French philosophers had a 'New Guinean' view
of women, who were looked upon as dangerous because of their
uncontrolled power and as potentially defiling, and as a cause of
chaos (Bloch and Bloch 1980, p. 40). The whole picture does
rather recall Sherry Ortner's observations.

2

The claims that women are closer to nature or that they can even
be identified with it, as we have met them so far, are also on
occasion associated with a discussion of 'the nature of woman'. I
would like now to treat, however briefly, this last theme of 'the
nature of woman'.

Among all the differences of opinion which we have met
concerning the concept 'nature', it is still not clear what its
meaning is when it is applied to individuals. Generally, it is

assumed to mean the singularities, the inherent traits and the vital forces of persons, animals and things. It also includes an impulse to act which is inseparably bound to someone. On the other side of the coin is the idea of 'going against nature', referring to the negation of this inborn impulse (Merchant 1980, ch. 19).

It is not my intention here to continue my search by interrogating all the great philosophers of the eighteenth and particularly of the nineteenth century on this subject. It would lead us too far afield and would only, I suspect, result in 'more of the same'. But I do not wish to leave Rousseau before I take advantage of this opportunity to call upon a study by Silvia Bovenschen, who examined the works of authors from the eighteenth and more especially from the nineteenth centuries. Her study involved investigating the cultural history and the literary imagery used for 'the female'. Her book is entitled *Die imaginierte Weiblichkeit*, the imaginary feminine. Her topic thus involves femininity as it is represented in all forms of literature, and in art in general.

To Sigmund Freud's assertion that 'people have always "*gegrübelt*" [brooded over] the puzzle of femininity', Bovenschen reacts with the comment:

> Let that be the case, but then this '*grübeln*' [brooding] does not have so much to do with the real existence of women nor with the few theoretical discourses, but rather with symbolic presentations, projected sensations, in short, with women as the female bearers of male nostalgia. The '*grübeln*' always found its starting point in the results of fantasies, in usurpations of the feminine. (Bovenschen 1979, p. 68)

Bovenschen notes the major problem that the many publications, be they artistic or historical, are seldom or never concerned with the real and concrete history of women and with discrimination against them, but only with the images or characteristics which a particular culture attributes to them. The 'nature' of the woman is delineated and determined by the man's culture. It is not concerned with sex only but involves primarily 'gender'. For this reason she gives the first book the title "*Schattenexistenz und Bilderreichtum*" (Bovenschen 1979, pp. 17–63), meaning a woman's existence is played out on the shadow side of life, but is rich in images!

Bovenschen discovered, as she gradually became immersed

in numerous writings, that either a reduction theory or a complementarity theory is nearly always in use. We speak of a reduction theory when women are assigned their own place because they are so segregated and have their own interests. I think here of the title of a book by Elizabeth Janeway, *Man's World, Woman's Place*. Women are given their own 'reservation', their own 'niche in culture' within the larger whole (think of the 'women's' magazines!).

The complementarity theory involves the tendency which believes that women must provide what men lack. Their duty is to care for, to serve and to please the man. We have already seen this in Rousseau's writings. Although it is also possible to note a certain egalitarian trend in the Enlightenment, the tendency to accentuate the inequality of the sexes still has the upper-hand. We can see there a metaphysics of gender which argues for the existence of an unequal polarity by calling upon a 'higher will', thus raising it to the level of 'being'. This means that subordination belongs to the 'essence', to the 'nature' of woman. The woman is pinned down to her womanhood and not fully accepted as a person. Rousseau had already said this in *Emile*, 'the man is only man at certain moments, woman is woman her whole life long' (cited in Bloch and Bloch 1980, p. 27). And Max Scheler in his '*Zum Sinn der Frauenbewegung*' [On the Meaning of the Feminist Movement] illustrates this pithy sentence when he states that woman 'with the peaceful resignation of a tree stands in life before the restless drama of the male sex – always concentrating on holding tightly to the great, simple fundamentals unique to our own species-orientated existence' (cited in Bovenschen 1979, p. 27). Thus we repeatedly come across the static feminine and the dynamic masculine ... I again quote Max Scheler, from the same work: 'woman is the being which belongs more to the earth, is more plant-like, more likely to accept as a whole all she experiences and undergoes, she is led by instinct, feeling, and love much more strongly than the man' (cited in Bovenschen 1979, p. 29).

This stereotyping also takes the form of idealizing, as can be seen in Karl Scheffler's book *Die Frau und die Kunst* [Woman and Art], where he writes:

While woman remains wholly what she always was ... namely, 'nature', she expands organically – growing and developing in all directions at once as the foetus swelling in its space –, the man must become 'de-natur-ed' and must tie his growth to lower goals. . . . He must depart from the unconscious harmony of woman because he must sacrifice it to become willingly what she is without having to will it . . . (cited in Bovenschen 1979, p. 31)

Should the man want to admit this 'wholeness' into his life, he must concentrate on two 'objects': on art and/or on the woman. . . . In this explanation of the difference between the sexes, the woman appears, as Bovenschen puts it, 'as something undifferentiated, mollusc-like, pre-individual and driven by nature and the laws of the species'. Bearing children is not looked upon as an accomplishment or a task, but as a mysterious relic of dark associations with nature. Being taboo, it is never mentioned in conversation or else it is wrapped in mystery. This allows Scheffler to say, in his work mentioned above, 'God and animal come closer together in woman' (cited in Bovenschen 1979, p. 31).

So we see that 'the nature of woman' in the middle-class society being formed in that period amounts to 'resting in womanhood' (Scheler); the value of being closed (Scheler); a nature element (Scheffler). We are clearly not discussing any everyday, flesh-and-blood woman. It is equally clear that the exorcising of a female natural force manifests a desire rooted in the man, a nostalgia for a reconciliation with nature, for a non-alienating existence, which he has ideologically rejected and which he projects onto woman (Bovenschen 1979, p. 32). Scheffler concludes: 'The passive harmony of the woman is nature; what man consciously wills is culture' (cited in Bovenschen 1979, p. 32). and 'It is, therefore, characteristic that the man experiences the woman less as an individual than a species. He does not actually idealize the individual woman, but the concept of woman' (cited in Bovenschen 1979, p. 33).

So we see that the woman's nature is again associated with nature. And again we meet the two aspects of this which we have already seen. On the one side there is the beauty and – albeit unconscious – harmony: 'While man has been busy with his one-sided preoccupation with knowledge, he needs from time to time to be able to cast a glance upon harmony, so that he does not lose his confidence that his work in some way or another has to do with a "whole"' (Bovenschen 1979, p. 37). But on the other side there is nature, which, for the thinking man, is the object, the matter he has received; it is the natural material to be possessed and in which he may intervene. He possesses the primacy of the *logos* and therefore, in Scheffler's opinion, it is not surprising that the man, as soon as he begins to think about woman, must despise her, because in this thinking she is seen as something long subjugated.

What is arresting in this male thought process is that woman is still identified with nature, but with *natura naturata*, that is, in a passive sense; and not as *natura naturans*, in which nature itself unfolds at least organic activity. The passivity is seen as a vacuum, a cavern, as we see from Goethe's words, 'the feminine is the only remaining container in which we, men, can pour our ideals' (cited in Bovenschen 1979, p. 38).

This short selection of texts from the thinking about women by male authors should not blind us to the reality of the life that women lived. They established a feminist movement; they were actively occupied; they fought their fight for emancipation; they exercised the arts and studied the sciences. But they made little headway towards breaking down the way of thinking about them in the dominant culture; that continued, over them but without them. Meanwhile, we must not forget that numerous women had themselves internalized this thought and that it would require a great deal of time before they, critically and independently, could reach an understanding of themselves which would not alienate them from themselves.

We may therefore conclude that the thinking about women in the eighteenth and nineteenth centuries (and for a long time thereafter!) was based on the 'reality' of numerous imaginings. We are dealing with a mythologized reality which is idealized at one moment and declared demonic at the next. But the real, personal and social form of women is absent.

I end this chapter with a quotation from a letter which the French author Gustave Flaubert wrote to Louise Colet (27 March 1853). In it Flaubert says, 'Woman is a product of man. God created the female and man the woman; she is the result of civilization, a work of art. In the countries where every spiritual culture is absent, she does not exist, because she is a work of art in a human sense'; and he wonders, 'is it for this reason that all great general ideas are symbolized as women?' (cited in Bovenschen 1979, p. 43). If these words reflect Flaubert's observations of his own culture, then he has hit the nail squarely on the head.

PART TWO

7

GOD'S GOOD CREATION

In Part 2, I will proceed to theological considerations. We are faced with the questions, How have faith and Christianity reacted to the changes we have described in philosophical and scientific thinking, in particular, to the practical changes that have resulted? What has happened to God the Creator? Beneath these questions lie others: What does the Bible say about creation and humanity's relation to nature, and how have Christians read and understood this?

It is in any case apparent that we, in our time, are faced with a choice which we must make with full awareness; a choice, namely, between two directions which are presented to us. On the one hand there is the direction, as it is described by Fritjof Capra in his writings, towards a new view of the world (traces of which can already be found in the new natural sciences), in which the separation between humanity and nature which forms the basis for modern technology is put aside in order to make room for a comprehensive view of all that lives: humanity, nature and cosmos. On the other hand politicians, economists and technocrats in Western society speak of a change in the future. But with this they mean a still faster and more refined technical development, an automatization and computerization of humanity and society so that it can keep ahead, remain one step before the competition, stay in the race. What we have before us is thus a continuation of what we call 'progress', in which the problems which distress us will only become more acute: the ecological crisis; the increasing wealth and prosperity of the West (which even then does not include everyone living there!) in sharp contrast with the growth of poverty and dependence on other continents; increasing arms production; the nuclear threat, and many more.

Whoever, as Christian and as theologian, chooses for the first direction (and it will become obvious that I so choose) will first have to think deeply about the way things are going as they have appeared in our faith and in our theology. Only when this has been elucidated will we be able to understand the present situation, and from there be able to see where the future is leading us, what type of new life can be expected for all people, the whole world, nature and the cosmos.

First of all in this chapter I will examine the meaning of the biblical expression 'subdue the earth' (*dominium terrae*) and the various interpretations these words have received (section 1). Next, (section 2) I will survey four theological themes: creation and covenant; God's words and acts of benediction; the re-evaluation of the Sabbath; and the question of immanence and transcendence (in connection with monotheism and trinity). Finally (section 3) I will treat the meaning of the words 'sacrality' and 'sacramentality' as we use these terms when speaking of nature and creation.

1

When we turn to the Scriptures we read on the very first page, in Genesis 1, 'In the beginning God created the heavens and the earth.' This first sentence alone is of decisive importance. It is God who through his word creates from nothing. 'His' sovereign power creates, creates and orders, gives a place to each and all within the universe. This formulation is a criticism of all the diverse, then current, creation myths, in which creation comes from a primal matter or matrix and is the result of the joining of male and female primal forces. In the Bible, creation is freed of all forms of fertility and is seen as an independent deed of God alone, who orders with 'his' Word.

This creation is the work of six 'days' and is completed with the creation of humanity:

> Then God said, 'Let us make man in our image, after our likeness; and let them have dominion over the fish of the sea, and over the birds of the air, and over the cattle, and over all the earth, and over every creeping thing that creeps upon the earth.' So God created man in his own image, in the image of God he created him; male and female he created them. And

> God blessed them, and God said to them, 'Be fruitful and
> multiply, and fill the earth and *subdue it*; and have dominion
> over the fish of the sea and over the birds of the air and over
> every living thing that moves upon the earth.' (Gen. 1.26–28)

I am interested here in the injunction to 'subdue the earth'.
Humankind is obviously given the commission, the power, to
rule over the earth and to subdue it: *dominium terrae*. This text has
led to various interpretations, as early as the first Christian
centuries. An element which they had in common was that being
the bearer of God's image and the dominion over the earth were
related: it is only because we are the image of God that we have
received the charge to rule. It is interesting to note that Gregory
of Nyssa rejects owning slaves on the basis of Genesis 1. He
argues that humanity may only dominate spirit-less creatures, not
other people (Liedke 1979, p. 64). He belongs to those theologians
who believe that even after the fall this commission and the power
to carry it out remained undiminished.

Others hold that the fall had its effect on the *dominium terrae*,
damaging and limiting it. Humankind has lost this power and will
acquire it again only in the coming messianic Kingdom. But in
general it can be said that in the first ten centuries there was not
really so very much interest in this question. There was rather a
static view of the cultivation of nature and the earth which did not
always have a connection to the *dominium terrae*.

In the eleventh and twelfth centuries, this thinking was
accelerated, probably in relation to the revolutionary technical
developments, particularly in agriculture. The famous monk
Hugh, from the Abbey of St Victor in Paris, developed a
surprisingly new way of looking at things. In his well-known
work *Didascalion* (*c.* 1120), which was distributed throughout
Europe, he associated the technical developments with the idea of
re-establishing the *dominium terrae*. With an appeal to the first
chapter of Genesis, Hugh suggests that a norm can be found there
to which humankind can return. In addition to God's grace, human
effort to attain knowledge and experience also served this goal.

For Hugh of St Victor, this clarification of the connection
between humanity's vocation and its own effort was not made
dependent on human advances in science, but first of all on
God's promise of salvation and God's gracious activity. In the

expectation of the coming kingdom of the Spirit, however, humanity's science can make a contribution. And here we see that technology receives the character of a historical process as well as having at the same time an eschatological meaning. An element of dynamism enters the thinking process (Liedke 1979, pp. 66ff.).

It is in the person of Francis Bacon that – five centuries later – we will see a sharp turn brought about towards a view of nature which would characterize modern science for the following centuries. Bacon brings Hugh of St Victor's reasoning further, but in his own way and according to his own interpretation. In his work entitled *Valerius Terminus or The Interpretation of Nature* (1603) Bacon suggests that through the fall both the domination over nature and the knowledge of nature had been lost. Humanity is both able and obliged to regain it through its own effort. For the true goal of all knowledge of nature is to regain paradise, in other words, the return of the sovereignty and power which humanity possessed in the first stage of creation. In Bacon's opinion, the natural sciences will return to humankind its dominance over nature.

Liedke remarks correctly that Bacon inverts the biblical sequence, the gift of being God's image-bearer and then being the subduer of the earth. Bacon believes that if by striving for more knowledge humanity can regain its grasp on nature, it will for that reason resemble God. His motto 'knowledge is power' implies, in his opinion, that humanity's resemblance to God is to be seen precisely in this aspect of power (Liedke 1979, p. 67).

Such a way of thinking lies at the root of the aggressive trait of all further attempts at dominating the world. Instead of a responsible management of what is given, it now comes down to a systematic conquest of what is yet still undiscovered. A few years later we hear Descartes calling for humanity to become '*maîtres et possesseurs*', masters and possessors of nature. In the combination of power and capital (possession) which this brings about, God's supremacy over creation is put out of action as a matter of principle. The promise of salvation must be realized through conquest.

In this connection, Liedke notes that what is remarkable is that there was little or no protest against this reasoning and against the resulting state of affairs, not even from the theologians. While the Churches had risen in protest against the new view of the world discovered by Galileo and Copernicus, they hardly challenged the new view of humanity's dominion over the earth. Even the theologians defaulted, as we see from the references quoted in Liedke's book (Liedke 1979, pp. 69–71).

These, each in their own way, relate to the following reasoning process: God wants the machine because God speaks to us through the facts of history. God wants the progress in our history, and the new period comes from God. All technology expresses the domination of forms and with it the domination of nature. The old mythical word 'subdue the earth' is fulfilled in technology. God's command to the first people, that confers the higher values and resemblance to God on all human reality, is nowhere more literally fulfilled than in technology. For this reason we see in technology a glimmer of the first morning of creation. Technological labour is the expression of our participation in God's creative endeavour and is the continuation of God's acts.

It is not coincidental that all these quotations are taken from Reformed theologians, since the Reformed understanding of 'nature' has had to travel along a long road to reach an ecological theology such as is found in the writings of Moltmann, for example.

In contrast with Roman Catholic theology, which saw in nature and in the earthly reality references to God's immanence, and which preserved and respected the earthly, material reality in its sacraments, Reformed theology always trembled before nature and symbols of nature, as before a dangerous fascination which could adopt a demonic shape. The results of the fall go so deep that nature, by definition, is fallen nature (Brinkman 1986, p. 8).

'Creating is separating' is a good example of a Reformation saying which makes me think even more that it is only one side of the coin. We will return to this later. In any case, this expression fits perfectly with the Creator's 'six-day working week' in Genesis 1. We see there that divisions are made on the first, second, and fourth days. But God and the world must also be separated. God is transcendent, the world is immanent, not divine, and is handed over in trust to humanity.

But there is another separation at the basis of Reformation theology, the separation between nature and history. In his work *Glauben und Verstehen* [Belief and Understanding], the theologian Rudolph Bultmann distinguishes the Western Christian understanding of history from the ancient Greek understanding. In Christianity the history of humanity is as a matter of principle separated from nature. 'For history is the history of mankind. Humanity is not a part of the cosmos, but is fundamentally separate from the world' (Bultmann IV, pp. 94–101). According to Bultmann, there are two types of reality:

> One is that of the world in which mankind exists, which he objectively observes and which he can dominate through technology. The second reality is that of the historically existing man which is, as a matter of principle, separate from the being of nature. ... Man is not classified as a creature of nature in the causal connection of natural events, but ... is responsible for himself. That is to say: human life is history. (Bultmann IV, pp. 128ff.)

This is one of the many examples which illustrate how until recently the customary (Lutheran) theology followed completely the course set by Descartes' separation between humanity and nature. We see a '*Vergeschichtlichung*' [historicizing] of creation, a creation in history. The phrase 'God as creator and ruler' can find its legitimate basis only in humanity's existential self-understanding. In addition, we may not omit the interpretation of Karl Barth, who is frequently mentioned in modern discussions relating to the conciliar process. Barth looks upon creation as the 'external basis' of the (historical) covenant, and the covenant as the 'internal (inner) basis' of creation. The 'inner' is 'being'; the 'external' is the periphery. In this way creation becomes the beginning of the history of the covenant, and creation can only be understood in terms of the covenant, thus from history (Liedke 1979, pp. 74ff.). At a later stage Barth's position changed somewhat.

The views of the Old Testament scholar Gerhard von Rad are completely consistent with this line of thought (Liedke 1979, p. 75). He asserts that creation is soteriological, which means that it must be understood from the context of redemption. Creation does not belong to the central events of Israel's redemption history, but is its entrance. What we actually see taking place here is that history is being positioned between God and humanity on the one side and nature and creation on the other. The doctrine of creation is deduced from Israel's salvation-history, and nature has no independent status or meaning. This implies that we can only really experience creation in the covenant, thus only from within history.

This has shaped a form of division of labour: the natural scientists keep themselves busy with nature and the theologians with creation in the context of salvation-history. The price of this division is the separation between creation and nature.

In this theology emphasis is put on the confession of faith *that* God created the world, but not on *how*. The phrase in Genesis 'subdue the earth' belongs to this 'how' in the creation story; and it is therefore not surprising that this passage has received little attention from theology. Put more strongly, Liedke assures us that in 1972, when he first began his study of the *dominium terrae*, there was not one single monograph to be found in any area of theology whatsoever relating to this topic. He discovered that this term was even absent from the registers of the theological dictionaries (Liedke 1979, p. 81).

We need not be surprised, therefore, that many authors have addressed a severe criticism to Christianity, namely, that Christian theology and philosophy are the cause of the current ecological crisis since they have not included nature and the cosmos positively in their reflections. I think here of works referred to by W. Achterberg: of the American author Lynn White, 'The Historical Roots of the Ecological Crisis' (1973); of the German authors C. Améry, *'Das Ende der Vorsehung: Die gnadelose Folgen des Christentums'* (1972) (The End of Providence: The Merciless Results of Christianity) and E. Drewermann, 'Der *Tötliche Fortschritt: Von der Zerstörung der Erde und des Menchen im Erbe des Christentums'* (1981) (The Deadly Step Forward: On the Vandalization of the Earth and Mankind in the Inheritance of Christianity), and of the Dutch author Ton Lemaire.

I think that we have to take this accusation very seriously and also as theologians dare to face ourselves in the mirror, even though it is of course true that the whole complicated problem cannot be brought back to one cause. What has gone wrong with theological thinking, that creation theology, in particular in the Lutheran tradition, has become so lean and that nature is allowed no, or in any case too little, value?

I would like to refer here to four aspects which are important in illuminating and expanding our understanding of creation and covenant, and in developing a more complete creation theology.

In the *first* place, the first eleven chapters of Genesis are rather to be understood as a 'primal history' in general, and only then as a beginning to the history of Israel. We owe this insight in particular to the important studies by the exegete Claus Westermann. He shows conclusively (Westermann 1972) that in the creation stories we are dealing with a *universal reflection* on the existence of humanity and of the world. There is therefore no question of the election of a particular people (Israel) nor of a covenant with them. In this primal history the creation narrative and all that goes with it is intended for all people and for the whole world. In these stories it is possible to indicate points of comparison with other creation myths from among neighbouring peoples. Everywhere people have thought about the origin of humanity, of the world, and of the universe. It is true that God already made a covenant with Noah, his wife and his family. This has its own revealing value for us all: first God said, 'I will never again curse the ground because of man ... While the earth remains, seedtime and harvest, cold and heat, summer and winter, day and night, shall not cease' (Gen. 8.21–2). And then follows the covenant:

> And God blessed Noah and his sons, and said to them, 'Be fruitful and multiply, and fill the earth ...' ... And God said, 'This is the sign of the covenant ... I set my bow in the cloud, and it shall be a sign of the covenant between me and the earth ... which is between me and you and every living creature of all flesh; and the waters shall never again become a flood to destroy all flesh. (Gen. 9.1, 12–15)

We see that there has been a reversal in God's thought, with the result that God has hung 'his' bow, first his weapon, now as rainbow, a symbol of peace and reconciliation, in the heavens. It involves a covenant between God and all that lives, and there appears to be a distinct connection between the words God speaks in Genesis 1 and Genesis 9. Creation is an event having its own character and meaning, of importance to all people, and thus to be respected by us all. It comes out of the shadow of the covenant and becomes its own entity.

In the *second* place, Westermann asks that we give our attention to another aspect, namely, for God's word and act of blessing (Westermann 1968). Until recently, theology has mainly given attention to the God of Israel's redemptive and salvific acts that culminated in the sending of the Redeemer, Jesus, the Christ. Particularly in Reformed theology, the main accent has been put on this redeeming aspect, and specifically on the saving blood of Jesus. In our time, in which we are all focused on liberation from all types of repression, our attention is directed by preference towards the God of the exodus, to the liberating God who leads people out of slavery and puts them on the way to the promised land. If Reformed theology has given too little attention to God's act of blessing, the case is different in the history of piety and the traditional prayer of the Eastern Orthodox and in Roman Catholicism. Both the *Euchologion* of the Byzantine Church and the *Rituale Romanum* (earlier called *Benedictionale*) of the Roman Catholic Church contain an enormous treasure of prayers of blessing over persons and animals, fruits and meals, over buildings and tools. However important redemptive behaviour may be, we run the risk, in giving it our attention too one-sidedly, of overlooking God's act of blessing.

However, both are found side by side in the Bible; each has its own meaning and value, and neither includes the other (Liedke 1979, pp. 85ff.).

God's redemptive, salvific activity has always been experienced by people, by Israel, as an intervention, as an event that occurs once and is not repeated. I am thinking of the exodus in the Old Testament and of Jesus' mission in the New Testament. They are both related to one another, both are saving acts for the redemption of humanity and have further liberating deeds as a result.

The activity of blessing, on the other hand, has an aspect of permanence. We can think of a continuous activity that provides support and maintains life; and it has its own dynamism. This blessing includes the waxing, ripening and waning of forces, happiness and joys, birth and death; in short, a repetitive event whose basic substance stays the same. The root meaning of 'blessing' has to do with the 'power of fertility', and it has a concrete connection with fields, animals and people. It also includes the end of life, to make place for new fertility. We hear elements of the Greek *physis* here (Liedke 1979, p. 86). In Genesis 1 and in Genesis 9 we also read of God's blessing of fertility when God creates animal and people.

The structure of God's act of blessing is different from that of a redemptive intervention. It does not consist of a one-off event which is first announced and then produces results. What characterizes it is its constancy throughout history, its continuity. The collection of stories on primal history, that is, from creation until the tower of Babel, but also the history of the patriarchs and matriarchs, deepen the permanent fundamental relationship of human society and of life in creation. Of the many passages in the Bible which speak of blessings, it is striking that they are described in the form of the people praising God and not so often presented as divine words. We only have to think of the Psalms.

From this too we must conclude that creation is not a derived quantity, but an independent category. Gerhard von Rad, already mentioned above, also recognized this is his book on *Wisdom in Israel*. He discovered that in the wisdom literature nature can be understood as creation not only via or through salvation-history. At the end of the Book of Job, for example, God fires a number of questions at Job which are pure creation theology and which contain a whole systematization of creation. With this, creation and all its regularities and cohesion enter into human consciousness. Von Rad even speaks here of 'creation's self-revelation' (von Rad 1970, pp. 189ff.).

This relation of continuous blessing by God and the praise from humanity as reaction and witness to it, brings me to the *third* important aspect that has long been overlooked in creation theology, namely, the meaning of the Sabbath. Humankind is not only the image of God the creator, but also of the God who rested on the seventh day, recovered himself, and saw that all was good. For too long we have spoken only of God's six days of work and we have forgotten the seventh.

On the Sabbath creation reaches its fulfilment; it is the feast of creation and the true recognition of each biblical creation doctrine, Jewish and Christian. It is the fulfilment of creation in the sabbath peace that distinguishes the concept of the world as creation from that of the world as nature. It is the Sabbath that blesses, sanctifies and reveals the world as God's creation (Moltmann 1985, p. 20).

The Sabbath is there for the individual, but equally for the people as a whole and for the land. The introduction of the Sabbath, in the case of the sabbath year, according to Leviticus 25, is the condition under which Israel is entrusted with the cultivation and preservation of the land. All living things had to be ordered according to their proper relationships within the borders of creation, and this in such way that it becomes possible to preserve and support the relationships of natural and historical societies. Only in this way will cosmos and *polis* [city] become a home to live in an *oikos* [nest, house, home] for humanity. Nature is then no longer humanity's possession to dispose of as it pleases, but a home in which God's benevolent and inviting activity offers hospitality to all creatures. Humankind then becomes the guest and occupant amid the rest of the creatures, away from the deadly asymmetry between humanity and nature (Link 1987, p. 58). The sabbath commandment includes the whole world existing with God; and humanity's exercise of the *dominium terrae* now comes to mean the restoration of a broken ecological order and of a disrupted *shalom* [peace] and the dedication to creation's right to live as a whole, wherever this is threatened or in danger.

Moltmann argues that the Sabbath not only interrupts our period of labour and our way of life, but also reminds us of the sabbath year, in which the original relationship among people and between humanity and nature, according to the norms of justice flowing forth from the covenant, must be restored and set aright. This sabbath year in its turn refers in history to the future messianic period and is a preview of the coming world which already begins in the suffering, death and resurrection of Jesus the Christ. This is the reason why the resurrection feast is celebrated on the first day of the week, that is, on the first day of the new creation.

Just as previously a distinction was made between the redeeming God and the God who blesses, so now we will have to become aware of the distinction between the creating God and the resting God. For according to biblical tradition, creation and Sabbath belong together. God not only created, he also rested, looked at creation and rejoiced in it, saw that it was good, and rested from the work of 'his hands'. If we as human beings thus believe ourselves to be the image of God, this means that we are not only people who create, co-create, and make things, but we must also be able to let go of our work, to relax, and, finally, to recognize the whole creation as God's possession.

The Sabbath is thus the 'feast of creation', of the completion of creation. God, as it were, comes to himself in rest. But, says Moltmann, this 'resting' is not a separation from creation, but a resting with 'his' creation, in the midst of creation. The whole of creation is intended to exist before God's eyes. God and creation experience one another on the Sabbath because just then, in their rest, they are receptive to one another. We see here God's transcendence and immanence coming together. God returns to himself and at the same time remains united with his creation. In the sabbath rest God qualifies this day through its restful presence and invites humankind and the whole of creation also to seek rest, to come to itself. In the end it comes down to the cosmic dimension of the Sabbath.

A noteworthy element in all this is that no particular place or mountain or area is sanctified, but a period of time, which is there for the whole of creation, and is thus universal. Other religions represent the divine in images, Israel does so in time; the Sabbath is God's imageless presence. The Sabbath cares for the interruption and the rhythm of human existence; it calls upon us to remember God's eternal creation Sabbath, but also to remember the promise of the eternal Sabbath of the messianic time (Moltmann 1985, pp. 281–94).

With this, according to Moltmann, Israel has given us two archetypes of liberation: the exodus from oppression to the land of freedom, as an effective symbol of external freedom, and the sabbath as a restful symbol of inner freedom. The exodus is thus the basic experience of the active God, and the sabbath of the presence of God (Moltmann 1985, p. 289).

Moltmann speaks of a 'polyvalent creation community: when God inhabits creation, a bond of love is formed, a bond of participation, communication and of many other relationships all woven together' (Moltmann 1985). In this context he pleads for a theologically inspired expansion of the horizon; reality is greater than our so highly narrowed history between God and people. Reality borrows its dimensions from the divine trinitarian community's orientation towards the whole of creation, and on the other hand, from the openness and the receptive attitude towards the divine community on the part of a history which includes humankind and nature in itself. In this way nature becomes fully 'part of the drama' (Barbour 1980). As we have seen so far, the idea that humankind is the crown of creation is not without its risks. On the contrary. In the end it comes down to the kingdom of glory, the sympathy of all things, which encompasses humankind, nature and God in a network of living together.

With this I come to the *fourth* aspect, namely a shortcoming in theology that has perhaps contributed to a misunderstanding of the relation of humankind, nature and God. I am thinking here of the overemphasis on God's transcendence and on the monotheistic idea of God. Both aspects have unilaterally brought about an image of a God closed in upon himself, in no way at our side, and far distant from 'his' creation.

The Old Testament 'unreachability' of God, as an expression of his transcendence, once so experienced and described in order to avoid the implication that God as a matter of course could be put to use in humankind's self-interest, has now in a period of modern technical development become translated into a formal system of transcendence and immanence, from which nature's restless availability for human power and intervention has been deduced. Transcendence, once experienced as God's holiness, has now been interpreted as his being disconnected from nature and creation. From this it again follows that nature loses its sacral character and becomes an available object (Wiskerke 1987, p. 68). God becomes a theocratic God, apart from us and above us, closed in upon himself, instructing, administering justice, judging. Pastors who become aware, in discussions with people, of the pictures they have formed of God, know that such a God-image has by no means disappeared, even though there is an ever-increasing number of people for whom God is someone who works with them in their lives.

The monotheistic aspects of the idea of God have strengthened this even further. Moltmann objects to the image of the monotheistic patriarch who is provided almost exclusively with masculine characteristics. He points out that that view of God is not deduced from the authentic Judeo-Christian tradition. Rather, this tradition was pushed off course when it was assimilated into the Greek and Roman thought patterns. Greek culture introduced the 'apathetic' tint to the image of God and being, which developed into the idea that God was not intrinsically involved with the world; and Roman culture added to this the patriarchal aspect of the 'all powerful father'. This *patria potestas* emphasized power and dominance. And now we return to humankind as the image of God who can exercise power over the world and over nature (Moltmann 1980).

Moltmann wants to give '*Gott in der Schöpfung*' [God in creation] a broader, more meaningful place by subjecting this monotheistic relation of dominance to a critical examination. Using a messianic interpretation of creation as a starting-point, he wants to replace the monotheistically distorted concept of God with an authentic Christian trinitarian understanding. He wants to put the primary accent on the community of the three Persons, the reciprocal engagement, the movement of love from one to the other, and the openness for creation. All creation is in this view returned to the attentive glance of a dynamic loving God. For humankind created in this image, life means life in relation to and in communication with one another and with the divinity. We no longer have to do with a dominating relationship but with a relationship in community. Such a theology will not advocate a hierarchical or centralized ordering of God or of people together or of people in relation to nature (Moltmann 1985, pp. 16ff.; Moltmann 1980).

Moltmann notes that so far this Christian trinitarian doctrine has not been taken really seriously. Perhaps we do this *ad intra*, that is, when treating the loving dynamism within divinity itself; but we do not extend this to include God's activity *ad extra*, where creation is concerned. There God still looks too much like the all-powerful and absolute patriarch or monarch, continuing the pyramid of power. After all, the symbol of the Trinity did not work out in the social relations in the world, nor in our interconnectedness with the Godhead. In his earlier writings Moltmann referred to the image of the 'perichoretic unity' within the divinity. Perichoresis means an 'embracing', a feeling of solidarity with one another, a reciprocal permeation and a living presence founded on divine community. In an eschatological perspective, it means the 'Kingdom of God', the Kingdom of glory, the three-in-one divinity's presence in its whole creation. Heaven and earth become the habitation and the environment of the divinity (Moltmann 1985, p. 191).

This concept of 'perichoresis' as a dynamic solidarity and an involvement with one another plays an important part in

Moltmann's creation theology and has as its result a fundamental change in the relationship between the divinity and its creation. When we take this relational attitude within the divinity seriously in terms of its external activity, then this means that God has become open and inviting towards the world, and is involved with it and has not created it merely as a product, a nature and world facing him as a foreign object. We may rather say that this rational, dynamic divinity has opened itself to the world, and draws it into its own dynamism. God moves towards the world and makes it possible for the world to move in the direction of the divinity. In this way, God's creation becomes an open system when applied to cosmic history.

God's living presence in creation implies that God, as cosmic Spirit, enters creation, and does so as a creating, reconciling and sanctifying Spirit. Just as the Spirit is the bond of love and source of communication within the divinity, so also, in its cosmic role, it brings about a relational and reciprocal solidarity among all living things in God's creation. It is this Spirit which puts the world in motion on the path to its eschatological future and fulfilment. Creation is no longer anthropocentric, but rather becomes theocentric, for its goal lies in final union and harmony with the divinity. We can again see God and the world, humanity and cosmos, in one great interrelated whole. It will now have become clear that an approach of this kind leads to respect for nature, which is no longer viewed as something mechanical to be exploited by humankind. God's living presence, the *vestigia Dei*, God's footprints, and the reciprocal solidarity of all with all, forbid this.

3

Using Moltmann's renewed theology of creation, which can also correctly be called an ecological theology, I have tried to show how very great a 'turn' theology has taken, in part as a result of the crisis in which we now find ourselves. In the Roman Catholic world, it was primarily Vatican II (1962-5), in its constitution *Gaudium et Spes*, 'The Church in the Modern World', which explained in more detail the positive teaching on creation which Catholic tradition has always known and confessed.

An examination by A. Houtepen shows that Vatican II has put its view of the world in a new perspective. It sees the world (*saeculum*) as God's creation in space and time. All reality and all history are thus related to God. In this reality and in this history, God completes his plan and realizes his Kingdom. Creation, redemption and final completion are moments in one and the same historical process and are in essence interrelated. Creation and 'new creation' are overlapping and simultaneous thoughts. The Holy Spirit is assigned the essential role of orientating humankind towards the Kingdom of God which is already in the process of being realized here on earth, albeit fragmentarily and in part (Houtepen, *Theology of the 'Saeculum'*).

In this perspective, the incentive to be responsible for and to care for the environment is already on the way, since an eschatological faith in creation is a stimulus to practice in modern society. It is a matter of managing the whole of creation in justice (Ganoczy 1976, p. 120).

There is as yet no mention of the cosmic interrelationship between God, world and humankind; and the term 'sacrality' is nowhere used for nature. But in the newest theology, this term *is* used with regard to creation and ecology, alternately with the term 'sacramentality'. Because these terms are often looked upon in distrust, and indeed can often lead to misunderstandings, I would like to take a closer look at them.

The basic question here is about the tension between God's transcendence and God's immanence. In other words, we believe that on the one hand God is 'opposite' nature, that God is 'above' creation and is not subsumed in it. But on the other hand, God cannot be completely separated from 'his' creation; God is bound to it, but not to the extent that creation is completely subsumed in God.

We know that the biblical creation narratives are understood and looked upon as a criticism of attributing divinity to nature and to fertility. Creation meant separating and differentiating.

We also know that the great overemphasis put on this separation led to a godless view of nature, and then further to a catastrophic relationship to it.

Absolutizing God's transcendence and the godlessness of a world which was then left to its own devices (meaning abandoned to human domination), has proved disastrous.

For this reason, many authors, by no means all of them theologians, express the desire that people will again develop a feeling for 'the mystery of things', for the sacral in nature (Lemaire 1986b, pp. 284ff.). Or put differently, we see the beginnings of an intuitive awareness of the unity of all life, characteristic of the so-called 'deep ecology' movement and of holism (Steenbergen 1987, p. 55). Whereas the famous sociologist Max Weber presented *'Entzäuberung der Welt'*, the demystification of the world, thus also of nature, as a characteristic of the process of modernization, now a desire for 'resacralization' is developing in the ecology movement.

It is to be expected that theologians are somewhat hesitant when they hear these terms, or that they may even fear them or totally reject them. Brinkman, for example, argues that there can be no question of a theology of nature, for that would imply nature's deification. He wants to maintain the emphasis on nature's not being God, but he does not want to claim that nature is a dimension foreign to God. 'The desacralization of nature should still leave room for its relation to God. In addition to its own reality, its value, its secret, its freedom and eloquence short of the level of God, should be given a place in a "theology of life"' (Brinkman 1986, p. 74). He writes about 'life as symbol' and about 'sacraments as signs'. Sacraments are in any case more than symbols of life, for they would then be as ambivalent as life itself. They claimed to be salvific symbols which show us a way, which provide a point of orientation in our ambiguous existence. They also have to be a 'sign' that does not destroy the ambivalence of our colourful existence, but which puts our life against a background of the biblical narrative (Brinkman 1986, p. 81). In a later work (Brinkman 1989), he goes deeper into 'the interrelationship of creation and sacrament'.

Liedke also stops short of sacralizing nature, but he does speak of sacramentalizing, by which he means that we can see signs in nature of God's creation. He refers to a title by Christian Link, *Die Welt als Gleichnis* [The World as Allegory], and to an approach used in an article by Daecke: because God in Christ has – considered sacramentally – not merely entered into the flesh but also into the substance, this too is sanctified. This idea is particularly dear to the fathers of the Greek Church, and has been preserved and even cultivated in Eastern Orthodoxy.

Again, another author, W. Temple, speaks of 'a sacramental universe'.

Because the earth is '*des Heren*' (the Lord's), Dorothee Sölle also writes of the earth as holy, and means by this the sacramentality of the earth, its '*Unverfügbarkeit*' [unavailability]: the earth is not merely and totally at our disposal; we may not do with it whatever we please.

The tension between God's transcendence and God's immanence, God's living presence among us and in our world, can change into an overemphasis on either of the two poles. The one-sided God transcending the world has led to deism, as is seen among many natural scientists, among them Newton; the overemphasis on God's immanence in the world has led to pantheism, as with Spinoza. There *everything* becomes deified.

I think it is possible to find a middle way here, where nature is not venerated, but is respected even admired, an object of wonder (van Dijk, p. 177).

First of all, the term 'deification' is misleading: God is God and is distinct from the world. The word 'creation' alone says that the world belongs to God, is created, that it is entrusted to us and asks to be steered and managed in God's direction. The world can thus be sanctified, even as we as human beings can, and can point to God. For this reason I can evoke a a certain understanding for the sacral character, for the inner mystery of things. And certainly the term 'sacramentalization' of the world, of nature, is dear to me; the world as God's sacrament, as a sign of God's creating, redeeming and sanctifying activity, which, however, cannot be realized unless we take up our responsibility as bearers of God's image and allow ourselves to participate in this process and become co-creators.

I would like to add my voice to Moltmann's in his development of a trinitarian theology. He starts with a Christian messianic interpretation of faith in creation and involves in it both the cosmic Christ (Col. 1.15ff .) and especially the Holy Spirit, who is God's creative power in an eschatological perspective. Moltmann connects the God who transcends the world with the God whose living presence is in the world. In so doing he reaches a panentheism, the mutual involvement of God and world. I will return to this in the last chapter.

8

A NEW RELATION BETWEEN NATURE AND CULTURE

Care about the environment has run parallel to concern for the position of the working class and for the independence of women. Although I have started Part 2 with a re-evaluation of the theology of creation, such a sequence is, in fact, misleading. It is seldom or never that the Church and its theology take the lead when new situations of need and injustice arise. ... More often it is the people themselves who feel responsible for the state of affairs, for rendering justice to humankind and the environment, who send out signals and sound the alarm.

The time has come to direct the spotlight on to the ecology movement and the questions it raises. It goes without saying that we again meet the tension between nature and culture (section 1), and then the position of the positive sciences and technology (section 2). Next, I return to Fox Keller's study to see to what degree a new relationship is developing between researchers and the 'object' of their study, a relationship characterized not so much by a sexual metaphor as by a reciprocal love relationship (section 3).

1

The word 'ecology' means, literally translated: the science of houses (*oikos*), thus by extension the space in which we live. To put it differently, it is the science which studies the relationships and processes which bind every living creature with its environment (Liedke 1979, pp. 18ff.). In ecological research, it has, in any case, been discovered that in nature all things are related to one another, each thing has a relationship to every other thing. Every human intervention in nature which produces profit also has its price which may perhaps be delayed but which sooner or later will have to be paid. Therefore, we can also say that ecology is the teaching which studies the regulation of nature (Schroevers

1984, p. 53). It is a question of nature as a whole, as a cohesive system. Modern ecology's starting-point is that nature is always more complex than we can take in (Schroevers 1984, p. 72). Ecology is thus the study of the structure and function of nature where humankind is expressly seen as an element of nature.

When we let this description sink in, we immediately reach the question: Are we people no more than a part of nature, is humankind totally swallowed up in it? In what is commonly called 'deep ecology', there is a tendency to answer yes. Humankind is, then, an element of and subordinate to nature. All life is equal and equally valuable. This produces an ecocentrism which is a reaction to the anthropocentrism which has determined our thought and behaviour for centuries. In contrast with humanity in the centre, now nature is, and as an intrinsic value with a normative character for humanity (Zweers 1984b, p. 114).

But we can also choose another starting-point. Humankind is more than nature; we are also thinking, willing, feeling, differentiating and ethical beings gifted with moral awareness, who allow ourselves to be led in our behaviour by values and norms, and who are continually being faced with decisions. We are, in short, beings who make culture. Just as at first we made nature subservient to culture, a reversal can now threaten which would raise nature above culture, making culture subservient to nature. When humankind's ability to differentiate is despised, the result is not a relationship but a separation between people and nature (Zweers 1984b, p. 121).

We touch again upon the relationship between nature and culture, in order to do justice to the richness of both areas involved. We must not think in terms of devaluing what has up to now been dominant, culture, but must work to re-evaluate what has been dominated, nature. First of all we must be well aware that nature embodies an independent value far removed from any usefulness or instrumentality which humankind thinks it can impose on it. This demands a change of mentality and attitude, and requires us to undergo a long and patient process of re-education.

Zweers considers that the idea of culture being a human ecosystem is a way out of the stalemate, 'either nature or culture'. Humankind not only participates in the ecosystem as a biological creature, but also as a social, cultural and creative being. This will require culture to give up its monopoly on values.

What we will need first of all is an attitude of contemplation towards nature. This contemplation can have an altruistic character when, observing and enjoying, we are close to nature and are united with it. But it is also necessary as a first step on the way towards intervention in nature. Although culture may then mean an intervention, an interference in the way nature proceeds, it should in our time be based on a relationship of humankind to nature which respects the latter's own character. Our culture can only continue to exist if it is in harmony with the demands of the natural environment. Humanity is thus not reduced to a purely natural creature. Yet it is necessary that humankind does not interfere arbitrarily from outside, but rather from within, through participation in nature's regulation of itself, and in this way create culture.

We therefore speak here of a new ecological theory of culture or view of culture, in which culture is done justice to through being embedded in nature. In this view, nature forms the basis of culture and not the reverse. This latter is generally the case in practical politics, where the economy becomes the basis for behaviour towards the environment. There is a possibility of choosing responsibly between 'ecologism' (the absolutizing of nature and environment) and 'economism' (absolutizing the economy) (Zweers 1984b, pp. 126–30). On closer analysis environmental problems appear to be more than just natural science or technical problems, but are primarily social problems. Social, political and economic aspects are beginning to come within the horizon of the ecological movement. The environmental problem, as a social phenomenon, is a part of a given social system and is to be understood in the light of the historical development of that society. This must not be seen as an external cause, but as the problem itself. Yet even this is not enough. We still have to reach back to what lies at the basis of our social structure, our political system, our economy. At this point we see the importance of philosophy in the environmental field: what metaphysical, ethical, social-philosophical and other philosophical dimensions find their expression here?

While writing this book I was struck again and again by modern technology's Janus head. On the one hand it has caused the countless problems with which we now wrestle. On the other, it has itself contributed to a better understanding of them.

Thus the philosopher Kwee Swan-Liat writes that since the exploration of space has provided a new view of planet earth, as a cradle of life and of humanity, a new awareness has arisen. Only in the photographs made at the end of the 1960s from outer space, which showed humankind the whole planet for the first time, have we discovered humankind's and the earth's past, present and future as one great interaction. Only in co-ordination with the earth can humanity find an answer to the crisis of our time.

The dialogue with the earth, within the framework of life in space and time, can be referred to as co-evolution: that is the total process of 4.5 million years of geo-biological evolution, in which conditions in the outermost layer of the earth, the *geo-sphere*, gradually changed to such a degree that the generation and differentiation of life, the *biosphere*, became possible, and in the last stage, with the coming of humanity, this life reached self-awareness, the *noosphere* (Kwee Swan-Liat 1986, pp. 231–57).

2

After these somewhat more philosophically coloured remarks, I would like to turn now to the sciences, and in particular the positive sciences, and to the relationships which some scientists have developed with nature.

I think first of all of E. F. Schumacher, the author of the well-known book *Small is Beautiful* (1973). In it he does not reject the historical development of technology, but above all he shows the threat to humanity and the environment posed by large-scale proportions and the structural violence with which modern technology is applied.

Schumacher is not primarily concerned with small-scale activities, but with an economy of, for and by people. He tells of a 'Buddhist' economy: in the Buddhist eightfold path the 'correct way of life' – at the same time the 'correct maintenance of life' – is seen as an ethical norm. Economic values have to be in agreement with religious and ethical values. In his book *A Guide for the Perplexed* (1977), he formulates his criticism of Descartes and the logical positivists who limit 'true knowing' to what can be established with certainty. Descartes had declared that nature, as an object to be studied, was dead matter!

For Schumacher it becomes ever clearer that, with our linear thinking and lifestyle, and with our grasping for a never-ending progress, we will never get anywhere. On the contrary, we are heading straight for a catastrophe. For this reason many plead for a recycling economy and for a recycling technology, in which we can maintain ourselves in a durable ecological balance.

This linear thinking is characteristic of the dominant scientific paradigm which up to the present has been believed valid and which originated in the seventeenth century in the work of such scholars as Descartes, Newton, and others. The term 'paradigm' has already been used in the first part of this book; and it is time I defined it. The word itself is derived from the Greek 'paradeigma', meaning 'pattern'. It is used for a system of concepts shared and used as a model by a growing number of scientists to formulate problems and their solutions. When fundamental changes occur in the scientific concepts, we have what is known as a 'paradigm shift' (Steenbergen 1987, p. 51). The term was introduced by T. S. Kuhn, in his *The Structure of Scientific Revolutions* (1962), and has been used in recent years outside of strictly scientific fields. When a consistent whole of images, values and observations, providing a particular view of reality, starts to shift and change, we speak of a change of paradigm or paradigm shift (Capra 1988, pp. 19–20). The scientific paradigm valid up to now is, as we have seen, analytical (it takes everything apart, but does not bring anything together), reductionist (it reduces reality to empirically examinable facts), and dualistic (there is a strict separation between the knower and the known). Furthermore, it is based on a mechanical view of the world, whose symbol is the machine. A new paradigm enters when the old one is no longer sufficient.

At present, it is again the natural sciences which are signalling fundamental changes and renovations, and are bringing them about through quantum mechanics, the theory of relativity, and in other ways. As a result of this it has been discovered that the original mechanical paradigm has to be finely tuned. Physics has brought to light the relational character of fundamental entities such as time, space and mass, in the theory of relativity. From our familiarity with evolution, we have also been made sensitive to the 'environmental dependency' of physical regularity, and to the fact that humankind cannot regard nature with the absolute independence of an observer. Laws of nature are thus no longer universal principles, but rather 'achievements' in an evolving process. From quantum mechanics, which treats the behaviour of 'particle pairs', some measurements reveal, as it were, the existence of a supra-local orchestration. In other words: certain natural laws exist which create a connection between events taking place at great distances. We can no longer speak here of our well-known laws of cause and effect; it is a question of something intriguingly and surprisingly new.

All these new discoveries have raised the question of the object of natural science. Can we still speak of this object as such, as the external non-subject reality, as dead matter? Is the view of matter as 'empty reality' meaningful as such? Here the process philosophy developed by A. N. Whitehead and others can help us. His fundamental idea is: every becoming, thus also every physical process, is always an introduction of newness into the world; a transition from potentiality, from possibility, to reality. Such a transition presupposes a moment of distance, of decision, thus of subjectivity.

In this view subjectivity and temporality (time) become joined together. This means that all that is can only fulfil its function of externality (its being there for others) *after* it has been a subjective act of self-determination. This latter is not a physical but a metaphysical argument, but it does have important consequences for the *interpretation* of physics as such. It describes physics as the study of an externality which has been preceded by subjective decisions.

The results of all this are very important. In the first place, it narrows somewhat the initial distance between subject and object. Further, it makes physics again a spiritual occupation, not because it reveals the decisions of divine wisdom, but because it suggests a self-motivated reality. From this it follows that in nature the subject cannot be discounted (Steenbergen, Rietdijk, Munnik, in *Civis Mundi* 1987).

It will be evident that exclusively rational thinking, which is reasoning and calculating, instrumental and dominating, and amoral, is no longer sufficient for this new phenomenon. Modern one-sided awareness must therefore be transcended in the direction of a deeper and higher consciousness in which there is room for an attitude of contemplation, solidarity and participation.

With this the notion of so-called 'value-free' science also disappears, because the gap between 'facts' and values is closed; the facts were facts that had been constructed to suit a particular investigation, 'hard facts', in which the spirit had been extracted from things so that they would have no value in themselves. 'Facts' then coincide with nature, values with culture. Both of these have come closer together in the new developments, and are again related to one another.

After the demystification of the world, its remystification is now important, by which I mean an awareness that the world and cosmos are filled with mystery and a respect for this condition (Berman 1984, p. 15). By this I do not mean to refer to a desire for regression, a return to a pre-technological world, but to a sense of the present transcendent. This will make science and culture work in a less alienating manner.

For myself, as one totally inexperienced in all these areas of science, it is important that I can understand that the rectilinear series of causes and effects, beyond which, in fact, nothing has been demonstrable, has now been broken; that nature is not a determined system, but appears to be a living, moving, self-regulating whole; and that there cannot possibly be an absolute separation between the person studying nature and nature itself; on the contrary, in such a situation, the two will become involved in one another and will need one another in order to make themselves known.

I must of course, mention in this connection the name of Fritjof Capra, to whose work I owe so much. I am not thinking so much of the data and content of his work, but of his flexibility, his attitude of receptivity and searching, his readiness to exchange ideas, doubts and suspicions with other scholars or specialists, to listen closely to them, and then to continue himself to think creatively. I refer here particularly to his most recent book, *Uncommon Wisdom* (1988), already translated into many languages. This book is the result of a search begun in 1970, to include more comprehensive areas than strict physics, whose narrow borders as delimited by modern academic studies he far exceeded (Capra 1988, p. 11). In his book Capra carries on many discussions with scientists in order to test and deepen his many new insights. But he also carries on discussions with many people who have alternative visions of the future, among whom are remarkably many feminists. It is always a question of people searching for a connection between physical and psychic phenomena and who believe in a more holistic view in science and in the approach to its application.

For the rest, I know that physicists have a great fear of the overly hasty analogies which holistically orientated people construct between mathematical logical models borrowed from physics and the social-psychological relations in human society and in metaphysics (Bennema 1987).

I would like here to mention briefly one example, as an illustration. It concerns the more holistic approach to health care in general, and to the treatment of cancer in particular (Capra 1988, pp. 139ff.). Capra starts then having learnt much from discussions with and the theories of Bateson and Simonton, from the conviction that living organisms are characterized by multiple and mutually dependent fluctuations. In such a model the organism is seen as being in a dynamic balance. Health is then a condition of flexibility in this balance; and stress means loss of balance and of flexibility.

Later he discovers that even more is possible than this relatively static, still very mechanical-looking model shows. For that context is only concerned with the possibility that after a disruption an organism can return to a previous condition and can thus come again into balance, but no more than that. A second step seems possible, namely, from the theories on self-organizing systems in connection and solidarity with the working of the human spirit (Bateson 1973). The healing forces in our organism can be not only self-regulating, but the organism can also undergo a process of self-transformation and self-transcendence that coincides with the various types of crises and stages of transition, and which results in its reaching a totally new state of balance.

This last development is a result of and is influenced by a mental process which serves as the dynamism of self-organization. This implies that the organizing activity of living systems is always a mental activity, and that all its interactions with its environment are mental interactions. This mental process, the 'spirit', is, on all levels of life, immanent in matter; mental process and life are inseparably bound together. When we accept this, we defeat the Cartesian separation of spirit and nature. Both becoming ill and becoming healthy are integrated aspects of an organism's self-organization.

Being ill and being healthy are thus essentially mental phenomena, even when we are not always aware of it. Of course, we have long known of the psychosomatic aspects of our being ill, but now it is a question of a holistic, cyclical process in which a person with his or her health or illness has a great influence on a condition and its resolution, in this case the healing of the illness. The psychologist Diekstra, working for the World Health Organization raised the question in his recent Duiker lecture, 'How mental is health?'

3

In this context of the scientist's changing relationship to nature and the awareness of humankind's participation in nature – in which the absolute separation between humanity and nature, matter as object and the human scientist as subject, disappears – I return to the study by Evelyn Fox Keller. Her presentation of the sexual metaphors which have been used throughout history to portray the knowledge relationship between spirit and nature have already been treated in Chapter 5, where I limited myself at the time to the first part of her book, *Reflections on Gender and Science*. But her investigation continues because she is searching for an answer to the question why science has developed as it now has, and why it is associated with 'male' and 'objective', with 'autonomous' and with 'separation, distance, and aloofness' (Fox Keller 1985, pp. 73ff.).

She is thus no longer concerned solely with the legitimacy of the expression 'objectivity of science' as an aspect of the object itself, but is also concerned with the stance, the attitude, of the scientist and his/her very presuppositions. She therefore wants to investigate the interior world of the subjects and objects, to look more specifically at what takes place on an interior plane psychologically when the male scientist thinks of himself as objective and autonomous. To do this she investigates the inner dynamism which forms the breeding-ground of certain ideas about the self and the other, subject and object, male and female, which are characteristic for our time, and how these mutually influence one another. More precisely put: she wants to treat the psycho-dynamism of the cognitive, emotional and sexual development within the established context of social norms and values, and then she poses the question as to the way in which such differences influence our opinions of science. In other words: if another sexual ideology had developed (i.e. other attributes for the genders), would there have been a different concept and practice of science?

I can recommend that anyone interested in this subject read Fox Keller's book, in particular the second and third parts, which are based on a psychoanalytical argumentation and which, in my opinion, offer surprising and illuminating points of view. Here I will be treating only those elements which are of importance for the subject of this book.

In the first place, we can note that *objectivity* is an ideal which has for centuries been attributed to men, and thus also to a male science.

> The demand . . . that a practical judgment must be correct and theoretical knowledge objectives . . . holds true in its form and according to its pretension, as it were, for the whole of humanity, but in *de facto* historical society is through and through male. Supposing that we describe these matters, which are viewed as absolute ideas, in one single word as 'objective', then we arrive at the discovery that the comparison objective = male is completely correct in the history of our race.

This quotation from the philosopher Simmel (cited by Fox Keller 1985, p. 75) speaks volumes. Objectivity is associated with reason, with *ratio*, and is suitable company for the 'hard facts' of 'real' science; subjectivity betrays an individual's own feelings of involvement, which are then qualified as 'soft' (Fox Keller 1985, p. 80).

From an interesting study carried out among English school-boys, it appears that artists are thought to be more feminine and scientists more masculine. In the attitude and work of an artist, feeling and eroticism may be expressed, but the scientist is strictly separated from these phenomena in his or her work (Fox Keller 1985, p. 82).

Fox Keller notes that objectivity is apparently linked with the acquisition of competence, control and dominance, aspects and attitudes which strengthen and maintain one another and which all lead to autonomy; at least an autonomy which is understood in a particular way, namely, as independence, freedom, and unrestrained self-determination. But there is more to be said than this static conception of autonomy allows. We could also have an autonomy in mind which has a more dynamic character. In that case we are concerned with an autonomy in which there is room for both the cordoning off of others (so that awareness of self can grow) and an involvement with others (which allows consciousness of the 'we' to develop). Through this latter the others also become subjects with which one has various aspects in common.

This reciprocity between subjects can only work when it is founded on a sufficient degree of competency in the 'I'. Only then can intimacy and independence be joined together. Only then can the fear of 'fusion' (which threatens independence) and the fear of loneliness and absence of contacts make room for a creative reciprocity and can rigidity be overcome by a fertile flexibility which expresses a genuinely objective attitude towards the world.

In other words:

> a dynamic conception of *autonomy* leaves an indisputable 'potential space' between the I and the other, the 'neutral area of experience', which, as Winnicot (1971) describes it, 'permits the temporary suspension of the border between the I and the non-I, necessary for all powerful sensations, sensations which make it possible to bridge creatively the distance between the knower and the known. It recognizes the ebb and flow between subject and object as the first requirement for love and knowledge'. (Fox Keller 1985, p. 104)

The ability to rejoice at another's autonomy is in itself already evidence of a balanced awareness of self that on the one hand is united with others and on the other can delimit itself from others. In such a dynamic autonomy there no longer needs to be a question of dominating another and of controlling. Power as dominance includes precisely an aspect of insecurity which produces, as a result, that the experiences of powerlessness are transformed into experiences of omnipotence. But a dynamic autonomy leads to power in reciprocity, and to reciprocal interest in and solidarity with one another, which can have far-reaching consequences not only for all types of human relations, both in personal and in public life, but also for the relationship of science to nature (Fox Keller 1985, pp. 104ff.).

After all this, the insistent question arises: What can this emotional dynamism mean for the acquisition of knowledge and the performance of research on nature? In the first part of this study we have seen that in modern scientific theories knowledge is in the habit of being associated with power and not with love, or with reciprocal merging.

Knowledge was thought to be acquired through an attitude of strict objectivity and by dominating the objects to be investigated. When we now look for a way to associate emotional categories such as solidarity and love with cognitive categories, we would do well to reintroduce these two categories into scientific practice. In this case, as they relate to the terrain of objectivity, they form a 'static' and a 'dynamic' objectivity.

When we describe objectivity as the pursuit of the greatest possible and most trustworthy possible insight into the world surrounding us, then such a pursuit can be perceived as dynamic when it is actively directed towards the common ground between spirit and nature, viewing them as a source for understanding. Dynamic objectivity aims at a form of knowing which guarantees the independent integrity of our surrounding world. It does this in a way which is aware of our solidarity with this world and which is based upon it. In this sense, dynamic objectivity coincides with empathy, a kind of knowledge of other people which is expressly directed towards what is common in feelings and experiences, in order to enrich understanding of the other's individuality. On the other hand, static objectivity is referred to when the pursuit of knowledge proceeds from a separation of subject and object instead of a disentangling of the two. The difference between static and dynamic objectivity thus lies in the presuppositions which one has about nature and methodology, and which have a decisive influence on the results of the search for knowledge.

Dynamic objectivity is thus the pursuit of knowledge which makes use of subjective experience in the interests of a more effective objectivity. Because it proceeds from continuity, it recognizes the difference between the self and the other (person or thing) as an opportunity for a deeper and more strongly articulated relationship. The effort expended on disentangling the self from the other (person or thing) is already a source of insight – potentially present in the nature of the self and the other (person or thing). It is a means of locating traces of hidden agreements and relationships. It concerns, therefore, a form of attentiveness, even love. For such a type of empathy, common feeling or sensitivity, an adequate sense of confidence is needed in order to distinguish between difference and continuity; put another way, empathy is based on a proper development of dynamic autonomy (Fox Keller 1985, p. 124).

The language and imagery some scientists use in this regard are also interesting and revealing. They are borrowed both from hunting and from the battlefield. I refer here to several examples cited by Fox Keller (1985, pp. 130–1). The biologist T. S. Painter thinks that research has much in common with a deer hunt: 'You have to be at the right place at the right time to meet your prey and you must, of course, have a loaded rifle in hand and know how to use it.' Or more strongly: 'With this meticulous unravelling research I wanted to follow the procedures of another's thinking in order to see how a relentless observer can grasp nature and wring it until it breaks out in a sweat and its sphincters relax!' It is just as if we were listening again to Bacon. . . .

From this aggressive language it is evident that there are scientists who still try to master and dominate nature as a whole or in terms of the separate objects in it, and this nature is thought of as woman.

Fortunately, there is a development in progress towards a multiplicity of images of nature and towards a variety of approaches to it. Daily practice appears more finely tuned than the imagery leads us to suspect. There are also scientists who view their acquisition of knowledge as something erotic. Michael Polanyi, for example, stresses that, instead of putting ourselves at a distance, we have the need 'To stretch out our bodies in order to penetrate [the object] so that we come to live in it.' And another scientist, Jane Goodfield, proposes that 'the best analogy of the practice of scientific research is always love'. For her, understanding is not the product of cool aloofness. She rejects passionately the metaphor 'which puts nature to the rack and tortures the answers out of it: "I find it a loathsome analogy. . . . It amounts to the same thing as rape. While science . . . differs from it as rape does from love"' (Fox Keller 1985, pp. 132–3). In the social sciences we find even more examples of an attitude of involvement, of conscious partiality and of self-reformation which brings the researcher to a more humble relationship towards the people to be studied (Risseeuw 1988, pp. 301ff.; Huizer 1988).

The discovery that nature is endlessly more complicated than science has thought, demands that a new attitude be adopted. It is no longer possible to classify everything and tie it down in laws, now that the natural sciences are discovering all types of regularities which are more complex, and of a greater variety than they had expected, and which interact with one another in various ways that cannot be organized in a hierarchical pattern. Reality appears to be more intricate than theory. For this reason a change is seen in the relationship the scientist has with nature; it is becoming one which tends more towards reciprocity. Such a relation asks that the scientist 'listens to nature'. This can lead to an exercise of the scientific discipline which is based more on respect than dominance; which on the one hand is not without power, but which on the other uses no compulsion and thus makes true knowledge possible. In a new relation between 'spirit' and 'nature', we can appreciate interactive descriptions which do justice to a view of nature which is ordered in its complexity and does not merely follow laws in a simple and rectilinear manner. From this it follows that two former dogmas, namely, that nature can be known and that it can be objectified, must be abandoned. The way in which we regard and observe things and the way in which we do research will have to be organized anew.

Fox Keller dedicates her last chapter, entitled 'A World of Difference', to the person and work of the American, Barbara McClintock, a world-famous researcher in the field of plant genetics, and a Nobel prizewinner, who had a difficult career because she diverged from the then currently accepted philosophical and methodological presuppositions. She continually felt like an outsider. McClintock was to a growing degree interested in the organization which appeared to exist in nature, and not so much interested in recording laws. In her view the understanding of nature can be reconciled with studying the differences in it. Exceptions are not there to confirm the rules, but have meaning in themselves. In this view the difference as such forms a principle in the regulation of the world which differs radically from the principle of splitting, or from the dichotomies: subject versus object, spirit versus matter, feeling versus reason, chaos versus law. Whereas these oppositions are directed towards a cosmic unity in which – very characteristically – each time, one element of the pair is excluded or marginalized (which then leads to one single comprehensive law), recognition of the differences in nature is satisfied with pluriformity as goal in itself.

This respect for the differences within a complex whole did not imply for McClintock the need for segmentation as an epistemological hypothesis, nor the need for a forceful, durable division in nature or in spirit or in the relation between the two. Division unbinds ties and imposes restrictions. But the recognition of differences provides a basis to proceed from a relational structure. It serves as a signpost for new connections and ties within nature, and as an invitation to become involved with nature. This attitude of respect for distinction asks, therefore, for a way of acting and of understanding which allows for the protection of the individual. McClintock would have liked to write a biography of each individual plant with which she worked! (Fox Keller 1985, p. 174).

If we carry this attitude over to human relations, we can draw important conclusions. Respect for the dissimilarity between people (all the 'others') and for our ability to empathize with them is also fundamental here. And this is the highest form of love, love which permits intimacy without ignoring the variation among people.

In McClintock's choice of words we often hear terms such as attention and attentiveness, to describe a particular way of thinking which expresses 'inclination toward', relationship and empathy. The point leaping to our attention here is that she has had the courage to abandon the frontiers between subject and object without putting science in danger. She has herself said of it that in a very intense investigation she became, as it were, more and more a part of the whole system, and felt herself caught up with it. Here we see a relationship between researcher and 'object' expressed in terms of intimacy, and attention as a source of knowledge.

It will have become clear that there are questions arising in this area for women scientists. In a science that presupposes that a named object (nature) is 'female', and parallel with this that the naming subjects (spirit) are male, every scientist who happens by chance to be a woman is confronted with an *a priori* contradiction in terminology and in imagery. From this arises a fundamental problem of identity: each scientist who happens not to be male proceeds along a way which on the one hand is restricted to an inauthentic situation, since one has to adapt one's 'self', and which on the other encourages subversion through resistance.

If a woman does not want to lose her self-awareness by colluding with a metaphor of the domination of nature as passive and feminine, she will have to search for radically different language and imagery. And these can only come about, as we have seen, in a new relation between spirit and nature. 'Listening to what matter itself has to say', and having a patient and attentive ear for the answers, can cause the growth of the conviction that we can only put our understanding of nature into new words and concepts when these come from the rich spectrum of *human* experience and are no longer limited to what our culture has called 'male'. We will therefore have to search for a science and philosophy which are not characterized by gender-specific associations, but by a wealth of different types of indications. In a new understanding of science, we are no longer concerned with 'taming' nature, but with 'taming' hegemony (Fox Keller 1985, p. 191).

9

ECOLOGY AND FEMINISM

After the frequently cited associations and stereotypes on 'woman' and 'nature', I would like in this chapter to look at the connection and occasional co-operation existing between the ecology movement and the feminist movement. In section 1 I treat the paths they pursue together, or those where the two movements encounter each other. Next (section 2), their spirituality comes under discussion, the mental attitude from which both perform their activities and formulate their perspectives. Both agreements and differences between the two are brought to light. I close with a few remarks on the term 'holism' (section 3).

1

Early in the 1960s two books were published in the USA, both of which had explosive results. I am thinking of Rachel Carson's book *Silent Spring*, which suddenly brought to the attention of a large public the already existing discussion on, and the concern for, the disintegration and slow destruction of the environment in the USA, and which also saw to it that the struggle for a cleaner environment was begun. Carson, an American biologist, had already written a study in 1941, entitled *Under the Sea Wind*, in which she denounced the harmful effects of DDT on the organisms in sea water. She has still more publications after her name, among them a poetical book, *Spring in Washington*, in which she describes the burgeoning new life and the singing of birds in the spring. A greater contrast than the one between this book on burgeoning spring and the imposition of a *Silent Spring* can hardly be imagined.

In 1963, Betty Friedan's book *The Feminine Mystique* also provided its share of excitement, particularly among women, and not only in America but over the whole world. She analysed the situation of women in America after the Second World War, when so many women who during the war had accepted all types of work in public life were sent back once more to house and hearth. The men had come home from the war, and 'of course' took up their jobs again. The feelings of uneasiness, the psychosomatic complaints, and the innumerable visits women paid to psychiatrists led Friedan to analyse and illuminate this situation. And we know that her book was not without its results.

Two woman who gave the start signal; two movements which were called into being, gathering all their forces, which are still growing, and which carry out important work and are also emphatically present in political life. Two movements, environmental and feminist, which in any case have had a number of aspects in common from the very beginning. In the first place a process character is noteworthy in both of them. The growing awareness of the environment would lead to a strong sense of alarm which would take shape in a forceful environmental movement. Next came a still deeper awareness of the motivation of this environmental movement: whereas initially it was concerned with 'how to survive' if the environment is disrupted, concern for the environment, for nature for its own sake, soon emerged and people realized that nature has its own value and that it deserves respect. Finally, there was an ever-increasing realization that all phenomena having to do with humanity, culture and politics, as well as nature and the cosmos, are interconnected, and that they are all mutually dependent and exercise influence on one another.

We see the same process taking place in the feminist movement. The awareness began with the analysis of the position of women in Western society. This concern and indignation brought women together to undertake action and launch a struggle, initially to liberate themselves from suppression and to acquire equally all human rights, and in so doing to shed their second-class status. Then there followed a deeper insight into social and cultural reality and of its structures which appear to be built on an ideology which was created around the female sex as the second sex. Later, the initially predominantly Western middle-class and white feminist movement encountered women throughout the whole world who were in an even worse condition. Feminism became at that moment a fundamental criticism of culture. Rosemary Ruether takes credit for showing in her work, as early as her *Liberation Theology* of 1972, the connection between the feminist movement and the environmental question.

There is still another element which the two movements have in common, namely, an egalitarian perspective. Women revolt against cultural and economic limitations which stand in the way of their developing their human potential as they would wish. At a global level, this comes down to a resistance to paternalistic thinking and patriarchal structures which only tell women 'what is good for them'. The feminist movement is a path which must be traversed from 'external determination' towards 'self-determination'. The environmental movement develops an ecological ethic which stresses the ties between humanity and nature, and which views humankind as participating in nature and no longer as dominating it.

From this it follows that both movements resist a hierarchical thought pattern imposed from above and oppose a linear thought pattern which arranges cause and effect in a straight line and which totally ignores the much more complex reality both in individual people themselves and in nature.

The goals of the two movements require new values and social structures that are no longer based on the domination of women and nature as merely supportive resources (which help the technocratic and consumer society to proceed according to plan), but on the complete expression and development of the talents of both women and men, as well as the preservation of the environment's integrity. Both movements critically oppose the costs of competition, aggression and domination which are the result of modern economy. Both movements have a subversive character, and both will have to become liberated from a one-sided, stereotypical 'gender' ideology which reduces both women and nature to 'wet nurses' (Merchant 1980, chs 6–16).

The characteristics listed here as common to both the environmental and feminist movements are already evident from a merely superficial examination. But during a closer study I was struck by even more phenomena, a few of which I want to mention here.

In the first place I refer to the way of thinking in utopias. It is remarkable how great a need there seems to be in times of insecurity and crisis, in which everything appears to fall out of place and one's own world feels unsafe and obscure, for a utopia in which people present the world as it actually should be. In the first part of this study we have already encountered several utopias, those opposing a mechanization of nature and those whose existence presuppose it. Here again we meet the same situation. Lemaire considers the feminist and ecological movements the most important manifestations in our time in the development of new utopias. He consciously relates this to

> Marcuse's appeal to dare to think in a utopian way as a sign of resistance to the spirit of the 'one-dimensional' affluent society which has neutralized this utopian imagery through the weight and prestige of its technocracy and the secretive ideology of its instrumental rationality. (Lemaire 1986b, pp. 258ff.)

From the various ecologically coloured utopias which Lemaire treats in his interesting contribution, I select that by Murray Bookchin, whose book *The Ecology of Freedom* was published in 1982. This is in fact not a utopia in the strict sense, but an extensive interpretation of the history of human society which results in an outline of an ecologically responsible society. His central thesis is that the will to dominate nature is the reflection of a social development when, namely, one person was increasingly repressed by another. The social hierarchy is then the cause of a basic model for the domination of nature. (And Rosemary Ruether already asserted in 1970 that the repression of the female sex by the male has been 'the' model for all forms of repression!)

In his travels through history, Bookchin shows 'how, through the Urban Revolution, the self sufficient neolithic communities with their relatively egalitarian relationships and their non-dominant relation to nature were overwhelmed and changed by civilization and its hierarchy' (Lemaire 1986b, p. 272). Bookchin's intention is not to plead for a return to the golden age about which in any case we know too little to describe it precisely. But his book *is* a plea for a society in which people are again involved with one another in mutual attention and help and in respect for unity with nature. Another interesting facet of his book is that its rewriting of history is unmistakably influenced by the feminist movement. Both in Bookchin's book and in Callenbach's 'Ectopia' (1975), women assume prominent positions in society. In any case Bookchin, and with him a number of feminist authors, believes that the position of women in the 'organic' societies of the neolithic period was considerably more favourable and more positive than in the civilization which followed it. The contribution of women to agriculture allows us to speak of a 'matricentric' society. When later a class society arose, patriarchal power structures had their turn.

> Men appointed themselves the priests (the former shamans) and warriors of society. The Mother goddesses and fertility cults were pushed aside by male gods who legitimized the new patriarchal order; patriarchy and civilization arose at the same time and meant, in Engels' well known words, 'a world historical defeat of the female sex'. The men not only try to dominate the nature outside but it is also the nature of women and nature as woman which must be tamed. (Lemaire 1986b, pp. 274–5)

This last sentence is in fact an accurate summary of the first part of my book, even though I do not seek there the support of possible matriarchal or matricentric societies, nor do the authors to whose works I owe my argument. Although I too believe that in earlier times there was not always such a strong and dominant patriarchy as we now know, I would prefer to base the present study on historically factual material. This does not mean that I totally reject all studies about matriarchy; on the contrary, I am curious about what these will produce in the end. I am thinking particularly of the important books by the German author Heide Göttner-Abendroth, who has, particularly in her recent publications, not only probed towards pre-historical matriarchies but also investigated the ramifications of the transition from matriarchy to patriarchy for numerous areas of life and science.

Now back to the question of the connection between ecology and feminism. From the joining of these two words a new 'direction' has arisen, 'eco-feminism'. This direction has the tendency to proceed from a specifically feminine nature and from woman's greater proximity to nature; it is inspired by a female or feminist spirituality which reinstates the goddess. In the last chapter I will discuss the snares and traps which are strewn along this path. In my opinion they lie at the basis of Stephanie Leland's views in her article 'Feminism and Ecology: Theoretical Connections' (Leland 1983, pp. 67ff.). But luckily various positions can be found among eco-feminists on this point. Although I certainly cannot agree with all the theses proposed by the American author Ynestra King, I can accept several assertions she makes to arrive at an eco-feminist policy, such as: (1) eco-feminists must design new models for human society which are in harmony with nature *and* (I would like to add) which contain a recognizability and power of imagery for women; (2) further-more, they must also struggle to forge as many bonds as they can among women from all cultures, races and classes, and over the whole world, in order to embrace and strengthen one another and to learn of one another's contexts; (3) and finally, King also recommends that eco-feminists develop empowering and imaginative forms of feminist activities, as they have done, for example, when they protested before the Pentagon against nuclear force. When I read the description of this protest demonstration by 2500 women, I was struck most of all by the period of mourning they had included in Arlington National Cemetery, where they placed gravestones for the victims of patriarchal violence. One woman even came from as far away as California to place a gravestone with the inscription, 'For the three Vietnamese women my son killed.' The insanity of war can be brought to light in no better way . . .

Finally, I would like to mention one more example of the connection between ecology and feminism, this time on a political level, namely the book *Green Politics: The Global Promise*, written by Charlene Spretnak and Fritjof Capra. These two committed people travelled through (the then) West Germany in the years 1982/3 to discuss and learn as much as possible about the organization, goals and concrete methodology of the German *Grünen Partei*, the Greens, the political party which wants to work explicitly politically for the benefit of the preservation of the environment.

One of the figures who seems to have inspired these people is Erich Fromm, whose book *To Have or to Be?* has been very influential in the process by which they became aware of, and later devised the lines and profiles for a new society. Fromm shows in his book how destructive it can be to put all one's emphasis on 'having', conquering and dominating. Instead of this he calls for a newly defined way of 'being' which leads to common experience, participation and exchange. In the conversations with many members of the 'Greens' there is a touching expression of an inner growth and changing view of society (Spretnak and Capra 1985, p. 54).

The authors held discussions around seven themes, which, it is true, are each related to one another but which each have their own meaning and value: ecology; non-violence; social responsibility; a grassroots democracy; decentralization; post-patriarchal perspectives and spirituality. These matters interrelate with one another in so far as they are all involved in a process. The Greens' policy intends to be a policy of transition; it does not want to be a goal in itself, but a means that, just like the visionary goal of an ecological society, is in continual development (Spretnak and Capra 1985, p. 56). The way forward will be determined more by quality than by quantity.

But – and here come the problems – it seems it is not so easy for feminist women to reach a good understanding and form of co-operation with the men in the 'Greens'. This is an example of a difficulty which we have been aware of for years: even in a progressive, left-orientated movement, a movement otherwise open to everything else, we cannot presuppose an understanding of the intentions, the perspectives and concrete suggestions which the feminist movement defends. On the one hand, the party, which declares that it opposes all forms of exploitation, is quite well aware of the exploitation of women in a patriarchal society. Their official programmes are certainly not sexist; and in the majority of the party's organs women are almost too well represented, right up to the leadership. But on the other hand, we find that the analyses of the different themes in their programmes, such as militarism, economy, health care and education, the feminist perspective is as good as totally absent.

This paradox is due to various factors. In the first place, the men in the party have too little understanding of the conviction of women that 'the personal is political'. They do not consider questions such as sexual violence, abortion and the like to be matters for hard politics, and therefore ignore them. Next, there is disagreement among women and men on the political style in which affairs are handled. The women consider it too aggressive and too competitive, while the men feel their political style must not appear 'soft' to outsiders in their competition with other parties. This causes tension between the realization of new and revolutionary goals within the party and the need to be taken seriously outside it in an identity which does stick out too much. There is an uncomfortable friction when one wants to establish a new policy and maintain the old style at the same time.

There are even a few men who are dissatisfied with this situation, but they have to carry on. The women are divided; many feminists just quit, being convinced that they can work more productively where they can work in a more authentic manner, while women who are less orientated towards feminism have no difficulty with things as they are. For Petra Kelly, the driving force since the movement began, the question is long settled, 'For me, feminist ecology is ecological feminism. They represent a holistic way of looking at things' (Spretnak and Capra 1985, p. 53). The disagreements also have to do with the difference in conception between the more visionary holistic 'Greens' and the (sometimes dogmatically) Marxist orientated 'Greens' (Spretnak and Capra 1985, p. 89). It is clear that the socialist utopia has lost much of its imagination and charisma by being too centred on the individual and on economic relations, by being as large-scale and technologically orientated as the capitalist utopia, equally inattentive to the environment which finds no place in its vision. There is still much to be ironed out, clarified and exchanged among the various 'tendencies', but a beginning has been made.

All those striving for a new society could possibly find meaning in the utopia of the Kingdom of God. This Christian view of the future, built on justice and peace, was announced by the Old Testament prophets and was realized in principle in God's incarnation in Jesus Christ. Every utopia is, as Lamartine says, '*vérité prématurée*' [premature truth], a truth which still has to ripen. But if we dare to believe in that Kingdom of justice, peace and love, we may not project it into an 'after-life', but the point is to let it inspire us here and now.

Joke Smit, a visionary of the feminist movement, has expressed the concrete content of this inspiration in a moving way in her well-known poem 'There is a land where women want to live'. The third verse begins, 'There is a land where men want to live', and ends, 'There is a land where people want to live'. Were the author of this poem still alive, she would certainly add a verse on our relationship to the land, to nature itself!

2

In the earlier chapters of Part 2 of this book, we have seen how strong the desire is for a more human society; for a greater connection between all aspects of life, and between our life and creation as a whole; for more empathy in the scientists' attitude towards nature. This desire has made itself felt in flesh-and-blood people, women and men, theologians, scientists and politicians, Christians and non-Christians. All these people are searching for a truly human quality of existence and for a spirituality which opens new perspectives. This deserves more attention here.

By 'another spirituality' I mean a spiritual attitude which provides a foundation for people's lives, which inspires them, and which colours and gives meaning to the whole person, our body and soul, our point of view, our work, our values and perspectives, and all our relationships. Spirituality is often seen in a religious context, rooted in faith and nourished by religious experiences. Contemplation is an indispensable part of it. But also outside faith and religion there can blossom a spirituality of respect for all that lives, for values which give life and are not destructive; of esteem for the particular elements in each individual person and in all that has been created.

Spirituality does not begin in an empty place; it does not just hang in mid-air or drift aimlessly. It arises in a given context, is based on certain values, and can be an inspiration for individual people but equally for groups and movements striving for a particular goal or moved by a particular ideal. Among such people are all those who have undergone a process of consciousness-raising during their lives, who have begun to look differently at themselves and the world around them, who understand their faith in a new way, and who have discovered a new way to live.

While this holds true for all these people, it finds its strongest and most emphatic expression in the writings, songs, drawings and personal witness of women in their process of development from '*Fremdbestimmung*' [determination by outside factors] towards '*Selbstbestimmung*' [self-determination]. They experience a transformation of such a thorough and radical nature that they first of all need time and space to assimilate it. With their new understanding of themselves they also look with new eyes at the

world in which they live, at their work, their relationships, and at
the religious traditions of which they are or were a part.

I am convinced that one of the reasons why the conciliar
process is so popular in some places is that it contains a call to
dedication. While the institutional 'Church' may, for many, have
become a difficult, stubborn reality, the biblical roots which lie at
the basis of this engagement have not lost their inspirational
force.

Moreover, we can become involved together shoulder to
shoulder, not only on an ecclesial ecumenical level, but with all
people who share the concern for justice, and with those who are
moved to act by their indignation at the destruction of our
environment. Where there is action, there can also be a place for
sensitivity, for the movement of the Spirit who moves where 'she'
wills.

All this can lead not only to the active participation of many
women but also to the creation of new possibilities for communication and co-operation between women and men which can only
bear fruit when they are based on a will to listen to one another.
All this will not cause culturally developed differences (the lack of
understanding and the stereotypes and prejudices) to disappear as
snow before the sun, but the warmth of a spirituality shared in
common can create an atmosphere in which we gradually live
beyond them and leave them behind us.

The context in which this new spirituality grows is determined
– in addition to feminism and ecology – also by the secularization
which is present throughout our whole Western culture, and
which sets before us new problems and challenges. Secularization
literally means 'becoming worldly', and is originally a juridical
term for the transfer of goods from the ecclesiastical domain to
the temporal. But when we now speak of secularization we
primarily mean the spiritual movement which arose as a result of,
and continued after the period of the Enlightenment (and thus
after the first great scientific and technical revolution), in which
humankind comes to stand independently and autonomously in
the world and is left to assume responsibility for itself. A too-
easily made appeal to God or ecclesiastical authority is no longer
acceptable. Humankind is returned to itself as a responsible
being.

This (perhaps too briefly described) process of secularization

has two types of results. On the one hand, there is the liberation
from compulsion imposed by ecclesiastical structures, and by a
misleading appeal to God's will; and there is also a purification of
false images of God. In this sense it is something to be positively
appreciated. On the other hand, this secularization has created a
spiritual and moral vacuum which can bring about both alienation
and meaninglessness, but which can also create a new space for
a new spiritual and moral orientation and for new religious
experiences (cf. Couwenberg 1987, pp. 45ff.).

I will first examine the alienation and meaninglessness which
secularization causes for many people. To do this I draw upon
Hans Achterhuis' essay 'De boom des levens: mythe of realiteit?'

Achterhuis starts with the observation that the tree of life has
an important place both at the beginning and at the end of the
Bible (Gen. 2.9 and Rev. 22.2). The tree of life is the outstanding
symbol of the mysterious association of life and death, of the
relationship between gods and humanity, of the unity of humankind and the earth. It is a symbol we meet in all cultures and in all
parts of the world.

What I am concerned with here is that Achterhuis clearly
shows that with the process of secularization the tree of life has
gradually disappeared from recent Western tradition, and with it
the experience of humankind's cosmic unity with the universe.
Thanks to our technology, the forests are literally dying and the
trees disappear.

Proponents of this way of thinking and experiencing, apart
from nature, are philosophers such as Sartre (who follows in the
footsteps of Descartes on this point) and Levinas (mankind is no
'homme-forêt' [forest creature]). But Achterhuis also draws attention to the role of secularization theology, which has also made an
important contribution to uprooting thoroughly the tree of life.
He refers in particular to a noteworthy work by A. Th. van
Leeuwen, *Christianity in World History* (1964), which is one great
attempt to interpret the biblical message in radical opposition to
all other religions, and thus to cut down the tree of life. According
to van Leeuwen, the tree of life, in the tradition of Israel, can
never be an extension of the mythological conceptions in other
religions. On the contrary, humankind is driven out of paradise,
out of its unity with nature, and is placed on the path of history.
Israel stands four-square against the powers in whose midst it

lives. For this reason van Leeuwen applauds so strongly in his book the development of modern science and technology, particularly as they relate to Judaism and Christianity. Together they will destroy what is 'ontocratic'. For van Leeuwen, 'theocracy and technology are allies, and together', according to Achterhuis, 'they will finally cut through – it is a wonder van Leeuwen does not call for an electric saw – the trunk of the tree of life everywhere' (Achterhuis 1985, p. 124).

Also in the 1960s, the well-known American theologian Harvey Cox put all the emphasis on humankind's own responsibility, and its duty to take its fate in its own hands independently of nature. He sees an opportunity to arrive at an exegesis of the creation of humankind in which the tree of life has completely disappeared. In Cox's writing too, the biblical world is cut free from nature, which has been secularized and given to humankind to rule over it (Achterhuis 1985, p. 124).

The emptiness and absence of meaning which accompanies this development is movingly illustrated in a passage from Sartre's *La Nausée*. There we read that the main character Roquentin is sitting under a tree which he has just discovered is dead. He feels it to be a real liberation that he is not an element of nature, that the tree is not a living centre of the world but is instead a dead thing. Humankind is here a pure individual, and is alone in the world. In this view, the tree's branches, although nearly dead, still reach towards heaven; but heaven is empty (Achterhuis 1985, p. 119).

But all this is only one side of the coin. Secularization has also created space for new forms of spirituality. It has become clear that it was precisely the making of humankind's own powers absolute, in order to make everything themselves, to take all life into their own hands – in short, to be their own lords and masters over everything and everyone (what Houtepen called 'a Faustian culture') – that brought upon many people feelings of discomfort and alienation. Their desire for the fulfilment of the deepest meaning of their persons, of their life and of the world, becomes increasingly urgent but is not satisfied. This is particularly true for many women, and for those among us who are concerned with the catastrophic disasters towards which the world seems to be rushing.

I would now like to mention a few of the characteristics

belonging to the new forms of spirituality which I see arising in various places.

In the first place, there is a growing concern for humanity itself, a concern for its humaneness and a desire to give it content again. What struck me in the conversations with the 'Greens' recorded by Spretnak and Capra was the attention necessary, also in politics, to human proportions: the struggle towards a 'technology with a human face', the struggle towards a form of society in which the individual person does not become anonymous and increasingly invisible to an ever more powerful bureaucracy, a mere number in the file. They plead for small-scale dimensions and for the restructuring of the economy on the basis of a democratic system which begins in human society (grassroots democratic economy). At the same time, they demand a society which does not exploit, which leaves people intact, including the people on other continents who live a life of suffering unfit for humans as a result of the businesses we build up here (Spretnak and Capra 1985, p. 90). I also include our responsibility for the future of our children, for the generations after us, in this spiritual attitude. Moltmann underlined this emphatically in a lecture delivered in Groningen (Moltmann 1988). But the 'Greens' also reject 'investments which have no future'.

To have been able to come so far, we have needed a transformation of our own consciousness which could only come from an acceptance of our own inner changes and growth, and from a new evaluation of the quality of a human existence which recedes before the present chase for quantity (of goods, of techniques, of profit).

In feminist literature about spirituality we meet primarily a resistance to patriarchal structures which still dominate society (and the Church). An uninterrupted line of domination runs through our world which restricts people of all classes, which will not allow them to become themselves, and which is based on obedience towards those who are 'above' and commands to those who are 'below'. This is a mistreatment of what is unique to each individual personally. Because women throughout history have generally been put 'at the bottom', they have had the greatest experience of this patriarchal hierarchical structure and they know that such a structure shatters the human consciousness into matter and psyche. It is a total misconception to believe that spirituality belongs only to the mental or the psychin domain, has nothing to do with the material, and therefore should be apolitical. At least this is the argument in a contribution from Antonelli. For her it is a question of being psychologically healed, and this by taking seriously the physical and material (the earth, the land), and by living in an ecologically responsible manner. For her these two go hand in hand, when she writes:

> If we want to survive the massive destruction which is the unavoidable result of male supremacy, then we must be in tune with psychic reality. Labelling spirituality apolitical and assigning it to another sphere than the material is short-sighted and nourishes the rationalist anxieties which are dedicated to maintaining the patriarchate. (Antonelli, cited in Spretnak 1982, p. 403)

For this reason Iglehart concludes:

> In the end, the goals of spirituality and revolutionary politics turn out to be the same, that is, the creation of a world where love, equality, freedom, and the fulfilment of individual and collective efforts is possible. If we join the two approaches to these common goals, we will also experience this fulfilment. (cited in Spretnak 1982, p. 419)

A second characteristic of a self-renewing spirituality is the growing sensitivity to connection, integration and interdependence.

We have already seen many times that not only does the patriarchal chain of command do no justice to the richness of existence, but also that the customary 'divisive thinking' analyses and devitalizes reality into fragments. It may have led to great technical accomplishments and extreme specializations, but it has done no good for human consciousness and the balanced development of the 'self'.

Moreover, it is noteworthy that people living in a period of great and far-reaching changes continually appear to have the tendency to leap from the one 'pole' to the other. They are more inclined to

> make absolute certain facets of human reality and to reduce the reality of human experience as a bi-polar field of tension –

> matter and spirit, objectivity and subjectivity, necessity and freedom, the rational and the irrational, continuity and change, the individual and the social, etc. – to only one of these poles. (Couwenberg 1987, p. 46)

It is obviously difficult to experience human existence as a bipolar field of tension and to preserve balance in it, even though in one situation the accents can of course be placed differently than in another. Those who feel this single polarity is a form of one-dimensionality desire a new integration of both poles: body and soul, male and female, immanence and transcendence, which can only work their way productively into human existence when they are involved with one another and integrated into one another. This growing awareness of polarities can lead to a balanced life even though the very fragile thread which binds the two poles can lead on occasion to an unstable balance and tensions in our existence. However, whoever severs this thin thread for convenience's sake regresses to polarization and retreats to the often aggressive bastion of one single pole.

In feminist spirituality the desire for the integration of body and spirit is great. Women have for so long been primarily consigned to their corporeality that they are now looking for an integration of spirit and body and for physical expressions of what lies deeply in their spirit. They try to avoid abstract and rationalist thinking and they prefer first to take their experiences seriously and only then to reflect on them and to give them a visible form. This makes me think of expressions in rituals and liturgical gatherings: dance, holding hands in a circle, signs of benediction supported by words.

There is also the conviction that the growth of the 'self' encouraged by preserving a connection with the diverse polarities not only changes each one personally but also leads to a transformation of groups and even a whole movement. In addition, making associations between the diverse visible phenomena in our society can help us better to see through reality and to discover its connections.

We can relate all of this to the ecological sensitivity which strongly emphasizes mutual dependence, not only in the structures of society but equally strongly in nature as such, and in the connection between society and nature. In this regard I must observe that many authors who are concerned with ecological phenomena are nearly always aware of and refer to feminism as an important trend related to their own movement, while many philosophers and theologians who also write about ecology nearly always ignore the feminist movement.

The mental attitude which proceeds from a shared unity and connection has also been called holism. This word is not as new as many think it to be. J. C. Smuts had already published his book *Holism and Evolution* in 1926. In it he offered a criticism of the reductionist and mathematical way of thinking prevalent in the modern sciences (Wolthuis 1986, pp. 84ff.). But it has become a familiar concept in the thought frame of the 'New Age' movement, and in particular with Capra. In addition to enthusiastic applause, it has also received its share of criticism. What I am concerned with here is holism's attitude towards life, the tendency to want to look at the whole and not only at each separate element; the tendency also to respect each individual part because it belongs to the whole and contributes to it. J. A. T. Robinson has observed that 'truth is two-eyed', and indeed whoever allows himself or herself to be orientated by the two poles, and thus uses both eyes, sees more and separates less. Nor is this limited to the flat expanse of our horizon, our world, however important it may be, but radiates out to the whole cosmos and to all that takes place in it.

Whenever this change takes place room can also grow for religious experiences and for a new ethical awareness based on a strong solidarity with everything and everyone. Stufkens, in his book *Heimwee naar God* [Homesick for God], describes quite movingly the paths his life has followed and the values on which his life is now based. For him the old images of God are antiquated projections that are no longer serviceable for him. Because he has been inspired by all types of new developments, he experiences God as the Eternal source of energy, the Absolute Consciousness, and the all-comprehensive Reality which we in ourselves can consciously become. Stufkens argues that in addition to a 'horizontal or sideways transcendence' on the social level (the surpassing of the self towards other people and society), we also need a vertical or upwards transcendence which nourishes our social activities through our unity with the universal life of the Spirit (Stufkens 1987, pp. 13–14). For

> if the social is not enlightened by an awareness of vertical transcendence, then its communality is in essence meaningless, as meaningless as is production and consumption for its own sake. Could not the absence of this transcendence be the deepest cause of the corruption of politics and economy, the extensive crisis in marriages and relationships, the frightening lack of motivation among high school and university students, listless performance in the work place, the gloom permeating many social groups and clubs, the emptiness of so many 'enjoyable' parties? (Stufkens 1987, pp. 87–8)

And Ransijn adds to this: 'If consciousness no longer becomes deeper, the spirit no longer grows richer and more ennobled, then society loses contact with its roots and becomes disorientated. Animation stagnates' (Ransijn 1987, p. 87). For me this last quotation summarizes very much. People can only be people in an animated reality.

Finally, I would like to mention a third aspect of this spirituality: respect for the 'holy' and reverence towards the All. In Western thinking a deep division has been created between the sacred and the profane. Proponents of belief in progress have seen the preponderance of the latter over the former as a 'victory'. Theodore Roszak, a well-known critic of our culture writing in the early 1970s, sees the dichotomy between the sacred and the profane as a fundamental problem which we must use all our energy to eliminate. He confronts three central concepts from the realm of the sacred: myth, magic and mystery, with three concepts from profane experience: history, technology and reason. It may well be true that history has become 'richer in facts', but it has become 'poorer in meaning'. We will again need all three 'old' aspects if we ever want to reach the ultimate secrets of our existence and also be able to celebrate them (cited in Van Steenbergen 1987, p. 54).

In feminist and ecological spirituality there is amazement and admiration for the unity and solidarity of all life. The life-force of cyclical regeneration and renewal is felt to be holy, healing, completing. Women come from their cyclical physical experiences to a resistance, shared by ecologically conscious people, against an explanation of the Whole in terms of fragments stripped of their interconnectedness. Therefore, (1) this new attitude leads to the creation of a way of life which is 'ecological for the person' (Anne Kent Rush, cited in Spretnak 1982, p. 383); (2) human and cosmic life is experienced as 'a dance of Being which we call Goddess' (Starhawk, cited in Spretnak 1982 , p. 418); and also, (3) the force or energy which brings about the relationship and interconnectedness between people, and between the person and the cosmos, is 'holy'.

This experience of the 'cosmic dance', the expression of mutual solidarity between people and the world, encompasses, as something 'sacred', the person in soul and body. What holds true for nature in general is also applicable to corporeality as the most evident form of humanity's being nature. Both Moltmann and Capra consider the usual instrumental and traditional vision of human corporeality held by our culture as the '*Innenseite der ökologischen Aussenkreise*' (the internal aspect of the external ecological crisis). A person should experience and inhabit his/her body unashamedly, just as he/she inhabits nature outside, by being open to the body's own receptivity and spontaneity (Wiskerke 1986, p. 197).

Women have emphasized this aspect since the very beginning of feminist spirituality, namely, in goddess and witchcraft movements. In contrast to the distrust of all things physical and sexual which is to be found in Christian religion and morality, they argue that sexuality is sacred, not so much because it is a means to procreation, but because it is a force which fills life with vitality and joy, because it is the numinous mediator for a deep unity with another human being and with the Goddess ...

> Sexuality is not an obsession, but it is the forward moving energy of the Goddess, each time it is created and recognized honestly – in simple erotic passion, in the unfathomable mystery of being in love, in a marriage where the partners are part of one another, in periods of abstinence and chastity, or in endlessly many other shapes which we will leave to the imagination of the readers. (Starhawk, cited in Spretnak 1982, p. 419)

All forms of superior strength or force in this matter corrupts and perverts the holy power of sexuality.

3

If we now look back over all that has been said here, a few
questions come to mind which can be summarized in the fundamental question: Are the words 'holism' and 'holistic' the best
terms to express the new outlook and the new attitude of the
environmental and feminist movements?

I will reproduce here three answers, each formulated from a
very different point of view.

In his book *Uncommon Wisdom*, Capra begins to discover
important differences between the holistic and the ecological:

> A holistic way of looking at things simply means that the object
> or phenomenon in question is understood as a cohesive whole,
> as the total Form, instead of being reduced to the mere sum of
> its parts. Such a way of looking at things can be applied to
> everything, for example, a tree, a house or a bicycle. On the
> other hand, an ecological approach refers to certain types of
> wholes, to organisms, or living systems. In an ecological
> paradigm the greatest emphasis is therefore put on life, on the
> biosphere of which we are a part and on which our own
> continued existence depends. A holistic approach does not
> necessarily reach further than one particular system, but
> according to ecological methodology it is essential to under-
> stand how a specific system is embedded in larger systems.
> Thus an ecological approach to our health will not limit itself to
> the human organism – spirit and body as total system, but will
> also take into consideration the social and environmental
> aspects of health. In the same way, an ecological approach to
> the economy will try to understand how our economic activities
> are rooted in the cyclical processes of nature and in the value
> system of a given culture. (Capra 1988, pp. 230–1)

A second answer comes from the 'Greens', who point out that in
Germany many people recoil from the word 'spirituality', and
even more so from the word 'holism'. They see a danger in this
term, that it could lead to a confusion with totality, and from
there to 'totalitarian'. And that is the very last thing they want!

I have also heard this objection from other people. Yet it rests
upon a misapprehension. The term 'whole' means 'interconnected', and is best expressed in the German word '*gansheitlich*'

[all inclusive], which is rather the opposite of 'totalitarian'. So long as this association is made, we should be careful with the term 'holism'. Moreover, there is – from a theological point of view – a totally different objection to make to 'wholeness', and I regret it sincerely each time I see a reference to the 'wholeness' of creation in connection with the conciliar process. 'Wholeness of creation' is a vision of the future, and as such an eschatological expression. It would be better to speak of creation's 'completion', a process on which we can work but which we, as imperfect people, will never fully realize.

Wiskerke's questions set out in a review of Moltmann's book *Gott in der Schöpfung* (1985) are also on this point. According to him, it seems as if Moltmann wants to make a mere harmonious rose garden of the world, and it makes him wonder where the thorns are, where the cross is. But, to do justice to Moltmann's work, he observes that in any case there are two fundamental aspects to be recalled which make the whole less like a bed of roses. In the first place, creation is still in between times, it has not yet reached its end; it is not complete; it has not yet reached its goal. And secondly, creation appears in a messianic light whose spotlights are the cross and resurrection, and is thus an enslaved reality in need of redemption (Moltmann 1985, pp. 73, 78ff.). Wiskerke concludes, therefore, that

> this messianic perspective forbids in any case a simple and massive identification of 'good creation' with 'existing nature'. As 'good creation', creation is more the final eschatological horizon than the factual totality of nature ... And furthermore, nature is not free of suffering and negativity. Under the present still unredeemed conditions, creation which encompasses both humankind and nature is bowed under the burden of death and mortality ... (Wiskerke 1986, pp. 198ff.)

10

WOMEN AND MEN – IMAGE OF GOD

We have now illuminated, from various points of view, the diverse images which Western culture has formed of both woman and nature. Furthermore, we have sought ways to reach a renewed interpretation of the meaning of creation and human-kind's relationship to it. Now we face the question: How does the Bible, and in particular the creation narratives, speak of humanity, and humanity as man and woman? (section 1).

In this way new perspectives can become visible, not only for woman, but primarily for man. Our Western society is for a large part based on the images of 'being a man' and of masculinity, which now come under discussion. The man's understanding of himself is also changing or can change (section 2). I close this chapter with a few reflections on the meaning of human sexuality (section 3).

1

All anthropology, even the Christian, has to take humankind as it now is for its starting-point; it may not study humankind from the pictures given by the creation narratives. This is the opinion represented in George Tavard's excellent contribution to a new Christian anthropology (Tavard 1973, pp. 187–210). Thus we must begin with the present, and then ask: How do people experience themselves, one another, and their relationships?

It is evident that over the past few decades the emancipation of all types of groups, and of women especially has caused them to reach a different awareness and has awakened in them a new understanding of themselves. The old patriarchal culture, the authority of the 'Fathers' in whatever social or ecclesiastical context, is starting to shake on its foundations, or else has already fallen from its pedestal. Dictates are no longer accepted, and the idea that 'Father knows best' does not work any more either.

Many people now want to consider for themselves what is special about their own existence, so that they themselves can shape it, can bear their own responsibility. This development is in principle good, and has its own dignity.

That it is accompanied by secondary features such as narcissism, individualism, lack of interest in others, lack of a feeling for community, is *not* good, and shows that the meaning of self-realization is not yet completely understood. If a person really wants to grow as a human being and develop, then this has to take place in a network of relationships in which giving and receiving work to promote humaneness, to shape the person. We live in larger or smaller communities of people who should work for one another's welfare. Moreover, we live in a world containing all the problems and disasters which confront us every evening on the television news reports. We must therefore also work for the welfare of this world.

We can only grow as people by living in relationships, by in-depth communication, and by orientating ourselves towards justice and charity. Through this attitude we learn to live in 'correct proportions'.

After these brief remarks, we will now turn to the biblical creation narratives, and first of all to Genesis 1.26–8:

> God said, 'Let us make man in our image, after our likeness; and let them have dominion over the fish of the sea, and over the birds of the air, and over the cattle, and over all the earth, and over every creeping thing that creeps upon the earth.' So God created man in his own image, in the image of God he created him; male and female he created them. And God blessed them, and God said to them, 'Be fruitful and multiply, and fill the earth and subdue it; and have dominion over the fish of the sea and over the birds of the air and over every living thing that moves upon the earth.'

Whereas in chapter 7 we were concerned with humankind's domination of creation (*dominium terrae*), I now want us to look at humankind's own creation, and at the meaning of this creation, that is, humankind as the image of God, and humankind as male and female. I now come to the question of what it means when we see it written that humankind is created 'in God's image and likeness'?

First, I would like to take a closer look at the term 'image'. We have already seen clearly how strong the human tendency is to make images for ourselves of others, and in particular images of 'the woman'. In so doing we lock people up in them, and it seems very difficult to let go of the images each time we see that they are no longer suitable.

This is equally true of the 'image' of God. To start with, we know from the Bible how strictly God was opposed to the making of images. In the revelation of divine presence on Mount Sinai we hear:

> 'I am the LORD [=YHWH] your God, who brought you out of the land of Egypt, out of the house of bondage. You shall have no other gods before me. You shall not make for yourself a graven image, or any likeness of anything that is in heaven above, or that is on the earth beneath, or that is in the water under the earth; you shall not bow down to them or serve them; for I the LORD [=YHWH] your God am a jealous God. ...'
> (Deut. 5.6–9)

It is clear that this prohibition has first of all to do with making idols. But it is equally clear throughout the whole Bible that we are also forbidden to make any realistic images of the biblical God who has revealed 'himself' to Moses in the burning bush 'I am who I am for you'. God is thus the fullness of Being itself, and this excludes every possibility of encapsulating God in space, time or experience. Every image would be an idol, a taking possession of The One who draws away from every definition (Duquoc 1985, p. 84).

Yet the Bible often speaks of God in images and metaphors, or else images are used in the words attributed to God 'himself'. But this does not mean that God *is* one of these images. Images, symbols and metaphors are there to highlight something, to bring about a recognition, never to nail something down. After the image has elicited a better understanding, we have to let go of it. Otherwise we will continually run the risk of transforming images, poetical or narrative language, into primary conceptual language, with all the misunderstandings to which this can lead. Poetical language is imaginative, sometimes also descriptive, but never prescriptive.

We must therefore keep a close watch on the context within

which this creation narrative was composed. The time was the exile in Babylon, where the people of Judah were removed *c*. 600 BC. Carried away from their country, they felt the danger of isolation and dispersion. But they still held tight to the experience of the liberating and redeeming God who led them out of Egypt, and so were able to make the leap of faith that this same God was also God the Creator, who, liberating and regulating, created this world. They had experienced this God as one concerned with the welfare of humankind and turned towards them, a relational divinity who spoke their language and linked 'himself' with them and their fate.

If then humankind is called the 'image of God', it expresses in any case a relationship between the two: a relationship of exchange between God and humankind, a relationship involving both of them. Whereas the older, more mythological creation narrative in Genesis 2 puts a stronger accent on humankind's earthly character (Adam formed from *adamah* [dust], into whom the divinity blew its breath and the powers of life so that he could become human and care for the earth), in Genesis 1, humankind's higher calling is revealed, created in God's image and likeness. For the possible meaning of the dialectic between 'image and likeness', I would like to refer to Irenaeus of Lyon, who, two centuries after Christ, was born in Smyrna but became bishop of Lyon. The same more mystically orientated vision will later also be found in the reflections of Gregory of Nyssa (Duquoc 1985, p. 86ff.). It is the idea of the 'creation of humankind as a divine process of birth' (Blommestijn 1988, pp. 86ff.). In this way of thinking, humankind is in a continuous process of becoming. As created people, we are *'capax Dei'*, that is, we 'turn to' God, we are receptive to God, but we need a whole life to orientate ourselves ever more towards God, to allow ourselves to be animated by the power of God's Spirit, and to be in God's likeness.

Only through this orientation towards the divinity do we receive the grace for a true autonomy which also makes us able to become as truly human as God intended. The creation of humankind is thus based on a relationship between the creating divinity and the created person who thereby becomes co-creating on earth and co-operates in God's work of salvation. It is clear that in this way of looking at things the doctrine of (apo)theosis so beloved in Orthodoxy, the doctrine of 'deification', comes into play. God's incarnation in Jesus, the Christ, plays a large part here. God has entered flesh, and it is just through this 'flesh-bearing' God, that we become 'spirit-bearing' people.

The well-known saying of Athanasius: God became human that humanity may be more like God, has also inspired and fascinated me for years, primarily because it concerns a process, a growth during the course of life which repeatedly confronts us with choices and which continually has to be filled in according to each one's personal life and context.

I would now like to return for a moment to the term 'image' of God. In Hebrew the word '*tsalem*' is used. In its oldest form it means image or representation, a duplicate. It refers in all likelihood to a familiar practice of ancient Eastern monarchs. Whenever they had expanded their territory further than they themselves could govern, they set up images of themselves to express their '*dominium*'. Therefore, if people are created, formed, and called to be the 'image of God', they are intended to be living representatives of God's royal rule on earth. *Tsalem* thus actually means 'representation'.

Earlier in this study we have seen the type of misunderstanding to which the words '*dominium terrae*', 'rule over the earth', have led. Obviously, the male interpreters of this 'ruling' as images of God have applied it to themselves and perverted it to *their* image and likeness. But now that we again realize that God's creative activity is not overwhelming and is not violent, that it is liberating and maintaining, a new light also dawns over our calling as God's representatives. All is transferred to us in order that we may protect it, may preserve and keep watch over the garden, may see to it that justice is done to everything and everyone.

By being a good representation, we can become transparent people through whom God's creative and caring presence can shine. I suspect that this is the turning-point in our process of being created to which Gregory, Irenaeus and Athanasius refer, and which moves us from representation to image, thus to 'deification', which means friendship with God as partner.

Next we must treat here humankind as man and woman. 'So God created man . . . male and female he created them' (Gen. 1.27). There is thus a differentiation in the image of God, namely into female and male. This sexual difference is the precondition for the future of life for the people and is the guarantee of God's promise that humankind will become numerous. Duquoc notes that classical Christian anthropology looked upon this sexual differentiation only as a biological necessity which did not influence a person's essence. Because in theological reflection women generally fell outside the field of vision, there arose a tendency in the culture of the time to describe being human according to a model of being male, and to view the woman as inferior or as a biological deformation. But according to Genesis 1.26–9, the 'essence' does not have to do with being man or being woman, but with their relation to one another. And this is the precondition for communication. *How* this relation takes shape is entrusted to the risk of freedom. How it develops throughout history depends on the reciprocal *becoming* of man and woman; and for that they themselves are responsible. Just as the visible aspect of this image has little to do with God (for God is a Name without image), so little does the differentiated image force upon us an 'eternal' model (Duquoc 1985, pp. 90ff.).

We can therefore posit that the first characteristic of humankind being the image of God, concerns humankind as *species*, and that this is true of each individual (female and male). Sexual differentiation comes only afterwards, is in the first place biologically tinted, and is in the text related to fertility. Life does have to go on, and the generations have to succeed one another. As was the case for the animals, man and woman are blessed with fertility; but no separate tasks or vocations are formulated for either the man or the woman. On the one hand, being male or female is of fundamental importance for the continuation of the human species and on the other hand it is of secondary importance in so far as each age and each culture gives its own meaning to being man or being woman. Or to put it in more modern terms: 'sex' was created, '*gender*' was not.

The way Genesis 2 has been interpreted historically has been quite disastrous as far as woman's subordination to man is concerned! But when this text is examined critically, according to modern scientific exegesis, it does not necessarily have to produce an androcentric result (Van Wolde, 1989; Bal 1985). Only through the creation of woman, *ishah*, can the man call himself *ish*. Man and woman each have need of the other in order to express their own identity. Only in the narrative framework of what is called the fall from paradise is there a question of man's dominance over woman. This was to be seen as the result of 'sin'. The author of this story sees that the relationship of this pair is not good. John Paul II has included this vision in his new reflection on women.

And now we must return to our own society and our own modern culture. Noteworthy here is that there is a whole range of connections between people which gives evidence of intimate relationship. The marriage relationship is one of them, and according to statistical studies it is one that is increasing. But there are also numerous lesbian and homosexual relationships, and relationships in society that are not marriages; there are also friendships between people who do not live together but who are deeply tied to one another.

An element which all these relationships have in common is that they are based on an experience of unity, love, tenderness, eroticism and sexuality. However different they may be, they all want to give expression to all these aspects; they are intent on seeing to it that each treats the other fairly, allowing him/her to develop as an individual, and that they grow towards one another. They see sexuality as belonging to God's good creation, and enjoy it.

Van Gennep correctly states that nowhere in the Bible can one find a doctrine which tells us how we must deal with love, sexuality and relationships (Von Gennep 1972, 43ff.). There are Bible stories which tell us how it can be, but none which tell us how it must be. Polygamy is a familiar patriarchal phenomenon, and cases of rape are also related in the Bible. These stories have to be left in the context of their own times. And if our social and cultural context differs fundamentally from it, we will have to form our consciences so that we can make our own responsible choices and decisions.

The reference to moral prescriptions, rules and norms for behaviour present in the Scriptures, even when they are presented as a commandment from God, or as God's will, or as a commandment from Jesus, have in themselves no power as evidence. The traditional Roman Catholic position on this is that God forbids certain activities because they are wrong, and not the reverse, that is, they are not wrong because God forbids them. God commands or recommends certain ways of acting because they are good, and not the reverse. (Beemer 1987, p. 132)

Yet I still think we can find an orientation in the creation stories which can shed light on all modern relational patterns:
– the basic relational structure of humankind;
– the caring and protective character of the relationship;
– the dedication to the redeeming work of justice and love, so that our relations do not become too strongly privatized, but are kept open to the world;
– the non-dominating but life-giving character of a relationship which benefits both parties – and many others. Here biological fertility is transformed and expanded into an existential fertility which is involved with the whole of life.

Now there remains the question whether we can even speak of the 'nature' of a woman (or by the same right the 'nature' of a man). I think not. Of course, we have been born biologically different, and I certainly do not mean to imply that this difference would have no influence at all on our psychic structure. This would be separating body and soul too much from one another, whereas they are essentially part of one another. But this process of our creation is so complex and is influenced by so many factors that it is not possible to decide on a strictly circumscribed male or female nature. On the basis of the current scientific state of affairs we can conclude that a person is not determined in his/her total structure by one single principle which shapes him/her as man or woman. This is already true on the level of their hormonal equipment, and it is true in a more complex way of a person's mental/emotional structure. Here so many different social, cultural and other factors play a role, that very often a composition of so-called 'male' and 'female' characteristics arises which can then change again during a person's life, during their growth and development processes. What it all comes down to is the emancipation of the person as person (cf. Korff 1984, pp. 365–7).

It is thus a risky matter to construct a natural moral law or a biblical anthropology on an abstraction of 'pure nature', a nature in all imaginable ordered forms of creation, without including humankind's historicity. Humankind is not a creature of nature, but a creator of culture. And for just this reason it is impossible to deduce moral norms, patterns of behaviour and natural characteristics from biological data (Häring 1979, p. 309). Rather, I suspect that the culture into which an individual is born is often so compelling in its customs and norms that we unconsciously internalize them and incorrectly consider them natural. Culture then has become a 'second nature'. We have to step back and look critically at it and reflect upon it so as to discover our own forms to support our own designs of life.

According to Schillebeeckx, the definition of being human is not given to us in advance – for Christians it is even an eschatological reality, and not one which can be realized in this life. People who have a complete blueprint of what it is to be human, a complete doctrine of salvation, have the tendency to develop a vision of totality which inherently leads to totalitarian behaviour. The teaching appears more important than the people for whom it is intended. Nature and the provisions of creation cannot provide us with criteria for what a liveable – because it is good – and felicitous humanity is, and thus what responsible behaviour means in terms of promoting human well-being. Nor can this be done by a so-called universal human nature which, as with a plant or animal, is intrinsically directed towards an essentially predetermined goal.

A person is a being entangled in histories. His/her *being* is itself a story, a historical event. Salvation and humanity, human integrity, is the very theme of a person's story. The critical force of human reason is also dependent on the historical circumstances in which this reason is placed. Human reason only beomes critical when it takes into consideration the ambiguous meaning of each period of history.

Schillebeeckx does see six anthropological constants as a 'system of co-ordinates for mankind [sic] and its salvation', which intervene in and condition one another, but which do not provide any concrete norms (Schillebeeckx 1989, pp. 672–88). It is noteworthy that he does not include among these six constants the sexual classification of people into male and female.

I have already argued above that any effort to form images of God carries with it the risk that we pin God down and limit 'him' to these images. I now have to add something to this. Given all that we can say about the being human of both women and men, it is also, seen from our position, risky to speak of God in predominantly male images, as if God were more male than female, and as if the female was not worthy to be used to portray the divine. If we really find it necessary to speak of God in anthropomorphic images, that is, images having a human reference, then the choice must be left open and must depend more on the context than on what 'belongs' to a particular sex. Not everyone accepts this; and the ecclesiastical teaching authority, and the theology upon which it is based, certainly do not.

The controversial article written by Cardinal Simonis, the Cardinal-Archbishop of Utrecht, in the periodical *Communio* is a good example of a different kind of reasoning ('Some Considerations on Feminist Theology', *Communio* II, 1986, 6). I will first summarize here a few of his propositions. In his second section he writes on the meaning of sexual references when God is discussed. He treats first of all a male image of God (2.1.1.):

> The image of a revealing God must *of course* – from the nature of God's relationship to creation – be male. For He is the Transcendent; He goes in an immeasurable way beyond the creation which, without compulsion, he has called forth out of nothing.

There is some discussion of God's immanence in creation and creatures, but the transcendence has 'absolute precedence'.

All that has been created has arisen from God's will to create.

> God is therefore owed primacy; He is the one giving life, while creation receives life from Him. This relationship is reflected within creation (by analogy) in sexual differentiation, in which primacy is the man's due. He is the one having the fundamental initiative in the unity of man and woman which is open to fertility. He is the one coming forward with his ability to become a father. The woman is fundamentally active as respondent, the one 'resting in herself' with her receptivity to motherhood, however indispensable the element she contributes to the creating of life.

Simonis quotes St Paul, who compares the relationship of man and woman to that of Christ and his Church, 'Man is head of woman as Christ is head of this Church' (Eph. 5.22–3). With this, 'primacy' is given a new meaning, because it now refers to 'a love relationship even unto death'. The responsibility of man and woman has, for each, 'its own character', just as Christ's life-giving love differs from the true acceptance of and co-operation with the life Christ gives. Simonis writes that according to some people the man is even the image of God's transcendence, and the woman is the image of God's immanence. In this human arrangement, the man is owed priority (which does not at all mean the same thing as 'superiority'!).

Analogous to the process of giving and receiving the life of grace, the man has a particular responsibility in the process of giving life which he can only bear completely and consciously through a participation in divine paternity. 'A female image of God cannot adequately express this primacy of paternity; the revealed image of God can therefore be nothing other than male.' Thus reads Simonis' conclusion.

In section 2.1.3. he again discusses the image and name of 'Father'. I quote:

> A special place in the above list of divine titles is reserved for 'Father' as it is used in the New Testament. That Jesus has made God known to us as Father is not without significance, because his fatherhood means being the origin. And this has its consequences for the fundamental arrangement between the sexes. Man and woman are both God's image and likeness, but each in a unique and specific way. Earthly paternity reflects, in its 'primacy' and irreducible fertility, God's all-surpassing fatherhood. For this purpose is man created.
>
> But God is also a protector of life. This is illustrated by another magnificent list of divine titles which were and are all too often neglected: Comforter, Helper, Consoler, Protector, Guardian. A woman, with her own responsibility and duty, can be an excellent image and likeness of the nourishing, sheltering, enveloping God . . .

again according to Simonis.

It appears to me that Simonis is guilty of circular reasoning when he wants to show that the male image of God implies the primacy of the man. His starting-point is man's biological primacy through paternity, which makes him life-giving and transcendent. This means that God's transcendence can only be expressed in male images. And from these male images, Simonis reasons back to the priority of the man, who thereby receives a theological legitimacy. What he is trying to prove (namely the priority or primacy of the man) is presupposed as already proven, and is used as the starting-point for his reasoning, instead of following it as a possible conclusion. The use of the expression '*of course*' (in the first sentence of 2.1.1.) is significant.

It is clear that Simonis looks upon the relationship between man and woman as a complementarity; this contrasts with the conviction which has grown among many of us that this relationship involves a fundamental and radical reciprocity. Also, on exegetical grounds, it is a mystery how he comes to speak of co-ordinating complementarity as *God's* concept (2.1.1.). Complementarity is a misleading and dangerous concept, because by describing the sexes as 'equal but different' both women and men are pinned down to 'natural' characteristics and stereotyped role patterns. It is also a static concept which does not take into consideration the changing cultural circumstances and the growth in each person's own life.

Seen theologically, I agree with Tavard that it is just in being God's image that we are called to transcend the limitations of the given situation; not by denying it, but by relativizing it and relating it to the state of redeeming and liberating grace from which humankind can live in a 'new creation'. From this, both woman and man derive their creativity. He also notes that receptivity is incorrectly called a female characteristic. If there is one single characteristic given to humankind which specifically marks its being a creature of God, it is receptivity and openness to the sanctifying and fulfilling work of the Holy Spirit. Mary is indeed an example of this believing receptivity but it is in no way specific to 'the woman' (Tavard 1973, pp. 195–201).

This sounds different from the presupposition which Hauke (Hauke 1982, pp. 183ff.) expresses (Simonis borrows extensively from this author), that the accent of female symbolism does not lie in its representing God but on making creation present. Receptivity is attributable to woman to a greater degree. For this reason she is in a certain sense an image of creation. . . . And so we find again an introduction of the association of woman with nature!

I do not intend to stay the whole time with the biblical creation narratives, however important they may be. Salvation-history has gone further and God has become human in Jesus of Nazareth. Incarnation means literally that God has entered into flesh, has assumed our human corporeality, and that God is close to us in the man Jesus of Nazareth. Because ecclesiastical teaching, in particular with regard to the admission of women to the priesthood, has put such a heavy accent on being male, the Church seems to confess God's becoming male (as opposed to [hu]man). This again ascribes a primacy to the man, this time in the sacral sphere, with the result that women are excluded from the priesthood.

In this regard Karl Rahner writes, 'So I think, for example, that the fact that Jesus Christ was a man – most likely something to which he himself gave no thought – is a simple fact which must be accepted. But we may deduce from it any general anthropological propositions' (cited in Röper 1979, pp. 66–78). The argument that Christ can only be represented by men can hardly have any theological force. It is, notes B. Häring, 'an idolatrous idea that Jesus would in some way be a male descendant of a male divinity. He is rather the full openness to the God of freedom' (Häring 1979, pp. 149–50).

In fact, Jesus places the people who believe in him in a totally new perspective: from being servants and immature children, we are called to friendship with God through the friendship which Jesus offers us when he says, 'No longer do I call you servants, for the servant does not know what his master is doing; but I have called you friends, for all that I have heard from my Father I have made known to you' (John 15.15).

This new perspective is conferred upon us through God's incarnation and through Christ's resurrection. Jesus not only restores the order of creation ('In the beginning' things were different), but also gives a new quality to our existence, sets a new order in motion which can be described as a life in his Spirit.

At Pentecost, when the Holy Spirit was poured forth on Mary and the disciples, the prophecy of Joel was fulfilled, as Peter says in his address:

And in the last days it shall be, God declares, that I will pour out my Spirit upon all flesh, and your sons and your daughters shall prophesy, and your young men shall see visions, and your old men shall dream dreams; yea, and on my menservants and my maidservants in those days I will pour out my Spirit; and they shall prophesy. And I will show wonders in the heaven above and signs on the earth beneath, blood, and fire, and vapour of smoke; the sun shall be turned into darkness and the moon into blood, before the day of the Lord comes, the great and manifest day. And it shall be that whoever calls on the name of the Lord shall be saved. (Acts 2.17–21)

Here it is a question of men *and* women!

The baptismal formula used by Paul in his letter to the Galatians (Gal. 3.26–8) is closely linked to this, and provides a view of the broader sphere into which the new order of salvation calls us: to live in such a way that we reach equal relationships between men and women, between whites and non-whites, between rich and poor, 'For as many of you as were baptized into Christ have put on Christ. There is neither Jew nor Greek, there is neither slave nor free, there is neither male nor female; for you are all one in Christ Jesus.'

In this same letter to the Galatians, Paul looks more deeply at the meaning of 'living according to the Spirit', and he lists a number of attitudes which are 'fruit of the Spirit': 'love, joy, peace, patience, kindness, goodness, faithfulness, gentleness, self-control' (Gal. 5.22–3). Whoever does not know any better could think this list to be a summary of typically 'female' attitudes. Those who *do* know better recognize in these fruits of the Spirit the fruits of a laborious process of conversion and transformation, which each person must undergo to avoid remaining stuck in his/her 'nature'.

It is therefore impossible to understand how Simonis can accuse feminist theologians of severing the Holy Spirit from the Trinity and misusing it. The list of divine titles he cites as neglected (Comforter, Helper, Consoler, Protector and Guardian) are just the images the feminist theologians use for the Spirit!

Finally, returning to the meaning of creation and its order, I would like to conclude that creation/incarnation/resurrection/

eschaton all belong together as one great process, and should not be separated from one another. The promise of the Kingdom of heaven is bestowed on us; we already live in the final times when we can believe in this promise and live towards it. We do not yet live completely in the final days, because of the incorrect choices we repeatedly make. And we make these often, also in relationships between women and men. But the promise has been made. . . .

3

When I stress so emphatically the need to humanize men and women, I do not mean by this that the differences between them are to be ironed away and that we are to ignore that we are differently equipped biologically. I am not concerned with sex differences, but rather with a critique of the 'gender' ideologies which so thoroughly determine our culture. What I keep in view is the necessary unfolding development of the positive potentialities in each of us, women and men, which is necessary in order to transform, to change the culture in which we live. For this reason I have already argued for a transformational model of the becoming human of men and women. By this I mean a model that is (1) directed at each one's being the image of God in his/her own person, with his/her own talents and possibilities asking for development, as well as (2) directed towards the transformation of society into a community with equality and reciprocity for and among all. The transforming aspect in the personal growth of each individual relates to the breaking free from prescribed roles and characteristics which are supposed to be either 'male' or 'female', and to a search for their own intrinsic and authentic possibilities which require shaping and development.

This does not yet suggest that the customary cultural attributions demonstrate only negative facets that we must discontinue. But it does say that we have to investigate critically whether these attributions agree with our own character and desire and, further, whether they have a positive or a negative influence on our present culture and society. No thinking person can doubt that this latter is necessary; but then the first is necessary in order to come this far (Halkes 1984).

Seen globally, the transformation runs a different course for men than it does for women. Women are expected to be caring, to be close to people, to display qualities of tenderness, feeling and intuition. This has led to a collective attitude among women over the whole world, and has produced a treasury of experiences and wisdom and human feeling. It would demonstrate an incorrect understanding of emancipation if women were to break away from and discard this hard-won attitude, as if it were something of lesser value. It is understandable that they have become allergic to being limited to it, because they feel themselves called to give shape to their responsibility for society and to be present in all structures and positions where decisions are made. What they need to learn is how to 'think big', to analyse structures, without forgetting the 'small', the relational and the affective. We have to keep asking: What does it mean concretely for people if this or that political measure or decision is accepted; and: Does it lend itself to the humanization of society?

For men the transformation is more complicated. On the one hand, they will have to evaluate the daily and small-scale more positively, so that these matters are not all left to women; they will have to share in the caring and relational tasks in the world, with attention for what is small and often unprotected. On the other hand, there is a need to come to a critical re-evaluation of modern culture, which still suffers from the dominance of patriarchal and hierarchical structures in thought and behaviour, and also from a dualistic thought pattern in which the so-called 'male' characteristics of achievement, competition, rationality and dominance are completely separate from the 'female' character-istics, such as process-guided co-operation and emotionality. Not only are they separated from one another, so that no reciprocal influence occurs, but the male characteristics have priority in our Western culture; they are in power, they are absolutized, and they have a dominant value.

During the preparation of this study I have noticed that there is a growing number of publications written by male authors who are dissatisfied with their one-sided socialization and with this dominant culture. In all honesty and authenticity, they analyse the way things are going and point out new paths. Feminist criticism has awakened them and made them realize just how harmful this one-sided role-attribution really is. They are mostly

American authors who use their own society as starting-point. But because we Europeans can also readily identify with these starting-points, their assertions hold true for all of Western culture. I mention here only two names: Eugene Bianchi (1976) and James B. Nelson (1988).

The first feature to which they draw our attention is that we live in a culture of violence; violence in all areas: war, mass physical violence in sport, sexual violence, scientific violence, economic violence, verbal violence. ... All forms, even the more subtle, have as their own (or at least as result) to demonstrate their power, to conquer 'others' or to dominate them, to impose their will on them, to put them in their place or to keep them there, to make them invisible.

I would like first of all to look more closely at a few examples, and then try to discover the cause of all this. To start with, there is militarism. Although right-minded people will no longer say so, I recall quite well the saying, 'War will make a man of you!' Nelson quotes a few statements from some highly placed American politicians and generals who made a direct link between waging war and 'masculinity'. President Theodore Roosevelt became the symbol of virile male conquest over physical weakness. In 1895 he declared that what Americans really needed was a good war, in order to make them men again. Roosevelt thought of war as the greatest test of moral and physical masculinity. And when the USA entered the Second World War, one government official offered the comment that America was again gloriously masculine. For indeed 'all real American men love to fight' (General Patton). Presidents Johnson and Nixon could not face the thought that they might be the first American presidents to lose a war, regardless of the consequences (Vietnam). Each of them characterized men who opposed hard and numbing militarism in terms which compared them to women or homosexuals, and thus something they found contemptible (Nelson 1988, p. 69).

A second example is the 'Super-Bowl culture of male violence' (Bianchi 1976) in American football. In his analysis of professional level competition, he recognizes four characteristics which propel the American violence machine: total lack of physical scruple; commercialization leading to high profits; an authoritarian, military mentality which thinks itself superior to all; and an expression of sexism. Bianchi notes that the roughest and most aggressive sports have the most success with the thousands of 'fans' who come to watch, and with the millions of television viewers. Each blow which eliminates an opponent is rousingly applauded, for only one thing is important: to defeat the enemy. Professional level American football confirms and strengthens the ideals of the male identity through its aggressive ethos. The real man is aggressive and dominant in all situations. Bianchi called the regular mass migration to the gridiron the 'weekly pilgrimages to the national shrines where the virtues of unscrupulous harshness and insensitivity can be renewed' (Bianchi 1976, p. 60).

Now that in various European countries we have witnessed the behaviour of soccer fans and the disaster at the Heysel Stadium, and have to pay the costs of extra policing to try to restrain the violence, we know what he is writing about!

It is hardly necessary to elaborate on sexual violence. It has been extensively discussed over the last few years, and it still continues. It is the violence of the older man, of the father, uncle, brother or neighbour, against a young girl, and of incest, which appears to be incredibly frequent. It is the rape men perpetrate on women who by chance are out late, or whom they know well, or who are even their own wives.

Further, it is becoming increasingly apparent that the 'pleasure' of rape lies not primarily in the satisfaction of sexual lust, but rather in the sexual humiliation of the woman. Nelson, from whom I borrow this, quotes a statement of a rapist:

> I enjoyed most of all my own aggression, that her body and life were in my power. She could do nothing in return ... My feelings were a mixture of sex and anger. I wanted pleasure but had to show I had power over a woman ... Sex wasn't very successful ... (Nelson 1988, p. 74)

The cultural anthropologist Peggy Reeves Sanday reaches the remarkable conclusion that rape is least frequent in societies where in addition to physical care, emotional forming and care are also strongly emphasized; and is most frequent where masculinity is identified with an ideology of toughness and dominance. According to her, rape is a way to hide male vulnerability and dependence: 'It is a man's defense against his own 'female dependence', a defense he shapes by degrading and punishing the female body' (cited in Nelson 1988, p. 74). This same mechanism also plays a role in the discrimination against homosexuals.

Finally, there is the violence of pornography. One of the most misleading qualifications is that this (literary) genre is called 'erotic'. Pornography has nothing to do with eros, because the latter is based on the interplay of mutual attraction, on reciprocity, not on depersonalizing and power.

It is typical of pornography that it reflects a power relationship and enforces the ideological humiliation of the woman. It is not primarily interested in nudity and sex, but in the humiliating of women, and in ever more sexualized representations of them. These images are distributed and bought for large sums. The buyers look on pornography as a way to kill time, and do not realize that something of it sticks in their minds. Male society has power over money, and thus over the media, and thus over the distribution of these images. And so we live in a 'pornographic culture' (Alice Schwarzer) that is given free reign in the name of freedom of the press. The entire community turns in derision against any form of censure. Free speech is a valuable democratic right which may not be infringed. But the question is whether this limited conception of freedom is in any way related to true human freedom. 'The battle against pornography is not a censure of what goes on in our heads, but a battle against the legitimacy of this type of publication' (Schwarzer 1989). Lucid and dauntless as she always is, Alice Schwarzer leads the campaign PorNo in Germany.

Susan Griffin has written a moving book on this subject entitled *Pornography and Silence: Culture's Revenge Against Nature*. The title is an accurate description of the content. Pornography silences women, and reflects culture's revenge against nature. Griffin speaks of a 'pornographic spirit' which dominates our culture, and expands this term to include all areas and expressions where one person dominates another and gives this other a lower, non-human meaning. She quotes from a novel, 'I use a woman like you as I would use a round hollow pot for another need.' She describes the attitudes of the famous British and American authors D. H. Lawrence and Henry Miller, who have an obvious physical love of women and an equally obvious spiritual love for men. Griffin also quotes from ecclesiastical decrees, where she untangles the 'pornographic spirit': man is the head of the woman, the woman is the body; or the woman is the (object) known, the man is the knower. In this way we are all shaped by the power of images, and by the experiences these images fashion (Griffin 1981, p. 4). D. H. Lawrence describes the growth of a woman as 'downward, as a root, to the centre, obscurity and the origin', and that of a man as 'growing upward, the stem on the way to discovery, light and speech'. This quotation describes exactly what happens in pornography. Woman asks to be subjugated to the man. Knowledge of her body is a forbidden obscurity, an unfathomable secret that can never come to light. The 'obscurity' of the female body becomes something threatening in this kind of thinking. A man who penetrates this darkness is in danger, he risks his life. The female voice, like that of Circe or Euridice, calls him back to hell or to death. She must be silenced and she must be coerced because the dark forces which she unknowingly keeps in her body are just as dangerous as the forces of nature (Griffin 1981, p. 13).

By making even children the objects of pornography, the child's innocence is violated, it destroys the lack of inhibition which the child's natural state had still guilelessly trusted. When children are misused for pornography, the child's body is deprived of its meaning, and becomes separated from its spirit (Griffin 1981, p. 254).

How do women react to this pornography and to the 'pornographic spirit' hidden in it? There are at least two possibilities. There are women who are forcibly misused; they are the victims. But there are also women who agree to be used for pornography. They make money from it and have internalized the pornographic spirit. In both cases the man/woman power structure continues to exist, through dominance on the one side and subjugation on the other.

I see an even sadder phenomenon in pornography produced by and for women today. I also think of the new periodical BEV, published by Leonie Greefkens. In an interview she announced that she thought it time for women to reveal their desires. She called that 'the last step in emancipation'. The woman's role must be made equal to the man's! I consider this a misuse of the word 'emancipation'. She feels happy she has never been a feminist, and every form of culture criticism is foreign to her. She thinks it bad to be separated from male society. That is why she produces her sex magazine. This sounds rather different from Alice Schwarzer ...

I am well aware that I have spent a good deal of time on this theme. But just because of its exacerbated nature, it provides an excellent example of an extension and a coarsening of the evil which so ravages our culture, the evil of violence, of the perverted anxiety for 'the female', and of the dark desire/urge to master and dominate women.

There is obviously something fundamentally wrong in the relationship between men and women, in male self-understanding and in male experience of women and the feminine. This is completely intertwined with male experience of sexuality and corporeality.

In this regard I would like to list a number of aspects of this tension, even though I am not able to treat them in greater detail in the framework of this study.

– First of all, the old hierarchical thought pattern plays a role here, the pattern which puts man at the top of the ladder, albeit under God. From this position he feels like the master not only of nature but also of woman.

– Further, women experience their body differently from men. They are more familiar with it, even if only through their experience of their body's cyclical behaviour; but also from bearing and nursing children. We would regress to a new form of dualism if we were to evaluate this biological data merely on a physical level. Of course, these events also include psychological experiences. Men are more ambivalent with regard to their bodies. When rationality, their 'mental' labour or their concentration on achieving goals take the upper hand, they lose contact with their body; it becomes more of an object, and especially an instrument. Another possibility is that a large proportion of men shut off their minds and give their bodies free rein, the result being an increase of violence, aggression, and a feeling of physical superiority. The integration of body and spirit/soul seems very difficult for them.

– Even more, the male would like to be immortal; he wants to be the hero who wins; he wants to leave behind achievements which will bear his name. (I am thinking here of the prestigious objects which several French presidents in succession have commissioned to be built during their administrations.) But he sees his body disintegrating, and for this reason he is ambivalent towards his body, towards decline, towards death. His ambivalence towards woman's sexuality also belongs in this list. For him she is something closer to the body, and 'sex is of the body and the body is of death' (Dodson Gray 1982, p. 25). Woman becomes for him both 'womb' and 'tomb'. For man, coitus is *'la petite morte'* [the little death], and I think women do not feel this way.

– All these experiences relate directly to the way a boy is socialized. In order to fulfil his role as a man, he must turn away from his mother and be introduced into the male world. This has a far greater shock effect than a girl's more harmonious growth to adulthood, which takes place in continuity. The man must be expressly non-female, must be independent, and must pursue his goal directly. Doubts and multiple interpretations are forbidden.

– This cultural 'condemnation' of men to a male world does not make communication between women and men any easier. When I say this, I am not thinking so much of young people who study together for higher degrees, and through their studies come more easily to exchange ideas. I mean here the average man and woman, and I know from discussions with such women how difficult it is for them to discuss 'deeper' things with their husbands, or to talk with men at their work places. Bianchi has written an important study on this subject entitled 'Psychic Celibacy and the Quest for Mutuality' (Bianchi 1976). He calls the inability to communicate 'psychic celibacy', and looks for ways to reach reciprocity. He describes this celibacy as an attitude which holds women both mentally and affectively at a safe distance; even coitus offers no opportunity for the interplay of tenderness, and even less for what goes on in the depths of each one. That this is harmful for both parties need not be argued. When you do not learn about one another's perceptions and experiences, you each live in a closed world and there is no open path to reciprocity. As an image in which modern masculinity comes to a high point, Bianchi refers to the Pentagon as 'America's model monastery on the Potomac'. He quotes Ibsen's *A Doll's House*, where the heroine observes, 'Your society is one of bachelor souls.'

For this reason we need to personalize sexuality in order to conquer fear, to transform vulnerability into communication (Ruether 1976). The sexual liberation of the 1960s did indeed free us from taboos and fears, but it did not reach as far as liberating women to be human beings. Whereas sex was formerly degraded by an exaggerated asceticism, the later libertarian attitude in its turn also deprived it of its own intrinsic and particular value. While at first we could speak of a suppression of the body, things later moved in the direction of a suppression of the spirit. The invitation to friendship, to love, to sharing one another's joys and sorrows, is still misunderstood or held at arm's length.

I can imagine that 'being a stranger' for one another plays a smaller role between partners in homosexual and lesbian relationships, and that expressions of tenderness and deep communication are more easily achieved. When we believe that men and women are not psychologically complementary to one another, and do not have to be, but that each is called in a personal way to grow and become fully human, then friendship, love and intimacy are excellent paths to realize these processes.

Taking everything into consideration, we must conclude that both women and men belong to both nature and creation, and also that they, each one and both together, have been called to create culture. The separation and opposition between nature and culture are misplaced, and have done much harm to our society and to the whole of creation.

What we now have to do to come to a more convivial society, where our living together is an expression of the new creation, where we strive to 'redeem the dream' and 'affirm the lost wholeness'. These are the words adopted by Mary Grey, and I gladly adopt them as my own. Because this is what it is all about.

11

' ... AND ALL SHALL BE RECREATED'

Having come to the end of a long and complicated search, we can stop and take a deep breath. To be honest, I am myself rather shocked by the discovery that the image of nature as a 'she' and of woman as 'nature' has proved so disastrous and is still playing havoc in our culture. In being associated with conquest, possession, domination, 'objectification', absence of spirit and passivity, with unpredictability and irrationality, the core of both nature and woman have been mutilated. And then I am putting it in a very abstract and inadequate way. . . .

The images still at work in our culture, either consciously or subconsciously, have not only damaged many women and our whole environment, but have also injured the relationships between woman and man, poor and rich, between peoples over the whole world, between nature and humankind. In short, justice, peace and the integrity of creation are at risk.

Greed, lust and an urge for power, as wise thinkers and poets have seen for many centuries, could very well be the roots of the evil which repeatedly plagues humanity, in however many different forms and contexts. And now these three seem to have joined forces again (cf. 1 John 2.16).

This journey into the images will, I hope, serve as a first step in their being dismantled; they have been dredged up from the unconscious and put under a spotlight. In this last chapter I will now make an attempt to call upon new images in which we can recognize ourselves, images which create room, images which surprise, inspire and invite. I know they will be images of a utopia, a not yet realised world. But we need utopias, and they have always arisen along the fault lines of our history. They are connections between faith and fantasy which attract us and encourage us to follow new paths.

Today is a beautiful day in May, and I have to write this last chapter. Suddenly I feel a pressing desire for a new clear space, for silence, for sea and wind and water. ... And I begin to dream. ...

I dream of the world, our world, as the body of God. ... If we may believe that God's presence in humanity became a reality in Jesus of Nazareth, we must also be consistent regarding its consequence. Jesus, the Christ, the risen, appeared to his disciples and told them, 'I am with you always, to the close of the age' (Matt. 28.20). If we believe Christ makes God present in his person, then with these words he is expressing God's continuous solidarity with the world. For this reason, the world can be portrayed as God's body. The basis for this is of course to be found in our faith in creation. Here I follow McFague (1987, pp. 60ff.), who wishes to link the image of body to Christ's resurrection and to the appearance, narratives. When the resurrection is interpreted in the light of these narratives, it becomes inclusive and occurs again at every moment. Then it is God's presence among us, God's redeeming, liberating and blessing presence *in* this our world. God's world becomes God's self-expression, the sacrament through which the divinity expresses her presence.

Earlier on we saw how in many organically orientated philosophies the human body is often experienced and described as a metaphor for the cohesion and intrinsic regularity of life. The body as image is by no means foreign to Christianity and the Church. In the Eucharist we celebrate the body and blood of Christ, that means we celebrate his presence among us. One of the images for the Church itself is the body of Christ. It expresses the solidarity of the community that believes in Christ.

But the Church is not a goal in itself; it is an instrument of salvation for people, for everyone. We therefore defraud the world if we only speak of God's presence when God's word is proclaimed or the sacraments are celebrated. Yet, we still have no image which puts the world outside the Church in God's presence. If we can imagine the world as God's body, we not only include all people, but also all structures in which people gather together; we include the whole of created reality.

Images can surprise, can spark recognition, but they can also shock. I, too, found this image surprisingly new when I met it in McFague's book (1987), but it also awoke in me a shock of recognition. For others it may appear an alienating image: a God with a body? But how have we imagined God the Father? Was that an image of God without a body? That seems even stranger to me. . . . If we want to portray our God as a personal God, the body is an essential element. For being a person means living in a network of relationships. Thus we believe our God is united with everyone and everything.

In any case the image of the world as the body of God belongs more to our time and is closer to our changing reality than that of the Kingdom of God. This latter image arose in a period in which the monarch, the patriarch, held sway and ruled. Even though we know something else is meant by God's dominion, it always has to be explained in order that it not be misunderstood.

Another objection may arise, namely, that God and the world would become coextensive, identical with this image. But then we only have to look at our own lives; we are not coextensive or identical with our bodies. Although we are intrinsically united with them (think of the expression 'embodied selves'), it is unique to humankind that we can think about our bodies; that we can relate to them in diverse ways; that we can give them the meaning we want. Thus we speak of a certain distance and distinction between body and spirit. A person is an animated (*animus* = soul) or 'en-souled corporeality', our existence is expressed in the unity of spirit and body; in this image God is also an 'embodied Self', animated corporeality, who endowed her body, the world, with breath and life, dynamism and cohesion.

God is thus not reduced to the world, but expresses herself in it. She knows the world from within, empathetically, and lovingly, a way of knowing which, as we have seen, is the most binding way of knowing. 'God so loved the world that. . . .'

Yet the world, as the image of God's body, remains a risky image, namely, risky for God. It makes God vulnerable. When I look around at the world, I receive two opposite impressions. On the one hand, there are individuals and groups who live in righteousness, who share, who help others, who behave carefully towards the whole of creation; and on the other hand, there are the violent ones, the swindlers, the wealthy who keep the poor subservient. In short, a torn world; and a fissure also runs through our own existence. It is a delight to see and feel the sun, moon and stars every day, but the rivers are dirty and the forests denuded.

The world as God's body? As risky as this image is, so vulnerable is God. And now we must add that this image also appeals to humanity, to our responsibility, to our will to be co-creative, redeeming and healing. To be the bearer of God's image means to represent God, to resemble God, to be God's co-workers and partners, treating the whole of creation respectfully and carefully. . . . It depends on us whether people, animals (yes, also animals), vegetation, in short everything entrusted to us, have the possibilities of existence due them, whether everything becomes what it is created to be. Whether or not the image of the world as God's body is to be an evocative and effective image depends a great deal on our willingness to take up and bear our responsibility in accordance with our dignity and vocation.

To refuse our co-operation in working for the world is not only a failure towards the world, but, because the world is God's body, it is also a sin against God.

Finally, and related to the above, this image can also strengthen the sacramental meaning of the world. Where righteousness and peace 'rule', and where creation is undamaged, there this world becomes transparent for the divine, there we live in God's presence. 'This is my body. . . .' But this image can only work beneficially and be convincing if people again make it a beautiful and valuable body, and continually take care of it. 'Then the world is no longer godless and God no longer world-less' (McFague 1987, p. 78).

This dream was so invigorating that, totally relaxed, I could turn directly to what now follows. On the edge between sand and sea a new dream of creation came upon me. I saw a glistening figure – I could not tell if it was male or female – who was working with chaos, creatively, orderly and watchfully. I do not know whether this happened during or after the Big Bang which took place nineteen billion years ago. But in any case, the chaos was still in motion and I saw too a large white bird, a dove, gliding over and hatching new life. The divine figure was bringing order to the chaos and assigning a place to everything, giving all that lived its own form, and then it discovered two strange figures. If these two were to fulfil their purpose, something special would have to happen. Therefore the divine figure blew her own breath and strength of mind into the pair, and they became people. And they were blessed and even addressed, for with them God had something special in mind.

In this dream there was no thought of a God creating from nothing, as a hero, only by 'his' word, but 'he' used what was at hand and gave it dignity. God did not create from nothing, nor did she give birth, but acted in love and creativity with what was available to her. Just as God gave the people the duty to watch carefully over the garden of life, to work in it and guard it, 'he' himself did this for the whole universe. Thus the whole of creation came from God's hands, and later she saw it was good and beautiful. It was a busy time indeed; and it remained a busy time! For God remained interested in her work, for after all, it was a rather complicated matter. But now and again God rested, enjoyed the sight, and rejoiced in it with the children of humankind.

When I awoke from this dream, I remained deep in thought. It was nearly dark, but I was still clear-minded; I thought, 'Why must we tie God down to certain images, and why are others forbidden?' Very different images pressed upon me. God: she is a dynamic, forward-moving force in the universe, an enticing, inviting Voice. He is my companion along the way, and the Beloved of his creation. She is a mother who defends her children when they are treated unjustly. God is indeed Love, a network of relationships in which we move, live, are.

And in Jesus of Nazareth, our brother, the divinity was so fully present and represented that we also have been able to see what it means to be full of God. A paradigm change took place in Christ. In him, through him and following him, we too can come to resemble God so richly and so deeply.

And then I again fell into a deep sleep and dreamed further. I saw 'the world as a dance festival' (an image borrowed from the novelist Arthur van Schendel). The cosmos was one 'Dance of Being', one great movement of all the living; it was an enchantment to behold. God's animating presence bridged all breaches and united all with all. The people were touched by God and also touched one another. God had blessed the whole of creation, and now they also blessed one another. Through the unity of God with 'his' body, the world, the people were not only united with one another, but also with the trees in their garden, the rivers in their land, with the forests near by. And all grew and blossomed. And the young calves were no longer boxed in crates, and chickens no longer imprisoned in egg factories. I could even dream of an *oiko*-theology instead of an *ego*-theology, in which God is freed of 'his' sole dominance and omnipotence, where the accent is put on the relation, the unity, the partnership. The whole physical reality was also in motion, a stream of events, linked together in a cohesive whole. The world was a dance; God and ourselves dancing together. . . .

After this dream, it was morning, a cloudy dawn, but the brilliance and joy of my extraordinary experience still lived in me. I had to return to my work room; this chapter had to be finished today. With a heavy heart I sat behind my desk. Where to go from here? Then I began to muse.

All at once I thought that if I were allowed to see the world as God's body, this metaphor would also include a reappraisal of the dignity of our own bodies. Our bodies would then be more than 'brother Mule', more than an instrument used by us Westerners and worn out by our active occupations. Then it would have its own intrinsic value and dignity. According to an old and meaningful saying in the Christian tradition, the body is the temple of the Holy Spirit. That means that we, in and through our bodies, are bearers of the Spirit, and that we must treat our bodies in such a way that this Spirit can shine through them.

It also means that the bodies of women and men have their own beauty, and that we may enjoy them with all our senses. Eroticism and sexuality also have their own value as belonging to God's good creation. We do not even have to use much fantasy here; there is a poetic story about it in the Bible, the Song of Songs. In it we hear the jubilation and delight of two lovers in total reciprocity, the characteristic of eroticism. Each of them is delighted in the other and makes the other a full participant. The garden in which they play is there in all its abundance of growth and prosperity, aromas and colours, and is the image of all sensual pleasure. There is reciprocal desire, and each one puts this into words, the man and the woman. The initiative for love comes sometimes from the one, sometimes from the other, and neither is the other's object or is overpowered by the other.

It is this desire for one another, and the passion that seeks union, that makes the erotic such an exemplary image of the human desire for unity with God. It is precisely the spark of our spirit-bearing body which inflames us and drives us towards the beloved other and towards the Secret of our existence. Bernard of Clairvaux writes, 'Jesus is the kiss of God which unites God with humanity.' We give this kiss when we kiss one another in love, tenderness and friendship.

From the very beginning there has been the relation, the unity. It is the basis of all our passion *and* all our *com*passion for one another. For over the sunlit garden in the Song of Songs, and stronger yet in the garden of Eden, there is also a shadow, a threat from outside, or from within one's own heart. ... 'The bitter puzzle of the good creation' remains. ...

If our body receives a sacramental meaning because it is included in the image of the world as God's body, then this is equally true of the woman's body as of the man's. So people with a female body must not be excluded from administering the sacraments, which are in a special way the signs and expressions of God's presence among people. This prohibition lies as a shadow over female corporeality, and all the arguments to justify it – tradition, Jesus' behaviour, Christ's maleness – are rationalizations produced by fear of the female body.

If I now think of all the inhuman images which hold sway in our culture concerning the 'threatening and dark secrets of female sexuality', I wonder whether we should not provide a larger place for eroticism, in all its aspects, than for 'culture' as a means of dealing with the 'naturally' given phenomenon of sexuality. Eroticism as a game of reciprocal friendship, beauty and the power of attractiveness. ...

Our body: the temple of the Spirit, the *ruach*! It has become a new and evocative image for me; but then it must be the body in all its fullness and vulnerability, in all its sensuality – in the innocence of the child, in the maturing of youth, in the richness and energy of the adult, in the invalidity of the handicapped person, in the decreasing strength of the elderly. An invitation to passion *and* compassion. . . .

Meanwhile, it has become midday, the sky has cleared and the sun shines, making all warm and glistening. A new fantasy comes to the fore: images of a conciliar process in which all who participate have come to a conviction that if such a process is ever to have a chance of success, then the unequal treatment of men and women must first be taken seriously. 'Women and men – image of God', was the motto of the 8 May Movement's latest celebration.[1] The conclusion of the present book is that this inequality can only be transformed into a justly shared power when we close the gap between nature and culture, when men no longer think of themselves as superior bearers of culture and no longer imagine women to be a passive form of nature to be dominated. If we are all a part of nature, of created reality, in short of creation, there is no imaginable argument to justify raising the one above the other. Humanity has indeed been filled with a unique breath of life which gives us our own responsibility, our own creativity to deal with one another and with the whole of creation. But unique is not the same as 'superior'.

Men and women, both participating in nature, both bearers of culture; both physically sensitive, both spiritually creative; both equally strong and equally vulnerable; both gifted emotionally and intellectually. Why should we then not each follow the path towards becoming fully human? The ways will be different, because we have different histories behind us. But at the points where on occasion our paths cross we can see on the far horizon the dawn of a more collective future which can lead to justice, peace and the inviolability of creation.

On the way to justice: this means dealing with people and with all life in such a way that everything and everyone is treated justly, that everyone is given the space to live that he/she needs. I dream of a technology which is supported in its 'progress' by an awareness of the true welfare of humanity. Technology now wants to bring us where many people do *not* want to go. I dream of another approach to economy and politics, which has now become so large-scale that no one can really understand it any

1 The 8 May Movement is an alternative, democratic and communitarian movement in the Roman Catholic Church in the Netherlands.

longer, let alone manage it. But, of course, I think first of all of
the many in our Western 'welfare state' who still fall through the
safety net into a marginal position where they live a caged
existence. And finally I dream that the rich West will turn the
debt which overburdens the 'Third World' countries into a debt
settlement of the same proportion, to offer some compensation
for all we have done to them over the past centuries. Of course,
with the result that we will have to adopt a more sober lifestyle. A
great conversion will be required of *all* of us!

Suddenly I remember the complaints from several women
which put a new light on the brutal injustice characteristic of our
Western culture.

It is still characteristic of our Western 'help' to developing
countries that it consists primarily of applying Western techniques
in farming, industry, transport and health care. The result of this
is a globalization, a uniformization on a world scale of Western
technological culture.

Whoever wants to know what mechanisms are active in such a
policy must make acute analyses. For Susan George of the
Amsterdam Transnational Institute, all analyses give the concepts
'power' and 'profit' a central place. They always ask, 'Who is in
control?' and 'Who profits?' Technology is never neutral, but is
the result of a centuries-long social and political process in the
West, in which the dominating class opted for technological
developments which worked to its advantage.

Whoever buys Western technology also acquires a collection of
social relationships which are closely associated with it but which
are nearly invisible. As George says, 'Western technology carries
the genetic code of the society which produced it.' But in the
mean time a country's own indigenous agricultural techniques are
crushed. George argues for support for a unique technology
adapted to Third World circumstances.

Valentina Borremans is of the same opinion, but expresses it
more precisely and concretely as it is applied to women. She asks
what effect the developmental programmes imported from the
West have on the situation of women. She pleads for the
development of a 'convivial' technology which confirms and
strengthens the quality of society. She mentions two types of
research: that done by the women themselves; and, on the other
hand, that which 'is done' about them. In the first case the

investigation is creative and practical and concretely helpful in improving women's lives. Noteworthy is that these studies are seldom dignified with the name 'research'. The other type of research aims primarily at improving women's productivity. It measures the 'improvements' in the women's 'welfare', but the question is, What do they mean by welfare? The two types stand diametrically opposed (Borremans 1983, p. 301ff.).

> Only when we see how the two types of research complement one another is it possible to find a democratic balance between the technical and legal regulations which will help women themselves to lighten the burden of their task and the others which reduce somewhat the inequality of women's competitive place in the rush for profit.

For many men and women the 'development' and 'adapted technology' only mean a modernization of their poverty and a new type of impoverishment for women.

For this reason I am in complete solidarity with the pleas recently formulated by these Third World women in the World Council of Church's journal *Women in a changing world*. They ask there: How is women's integrity threatened?' Their answer is that throughout the whole world men have a tendency to see women as things to be used, instead of considering them complete human beings deserving of dignity and respect. Their integrity is threatened by many types of dominance and violence. These women undergo an extra level of dominance by Western politics when there is a question of fertility, contraception, baby food and all such matters. The power to decide about one's own reproductive activity is a fundamental need for all women, a need which is again and again violated by the structures of both capitalism and governmental interference, and this attack is sometimes even aided by religion.

The Third-World women say, 'When sister earth suffers, all women suffer.' When land, air and water are polluted and poisoned, women and children, especially the unborn children, are generally the first to be affected by it.

And later I dreamed of the end of the culture of violence, of the end of its glorification in television, films and comic strips. I dreamed of the discomforting embarrassment young boys would feel if they had to sing songs during military training such as the one used in American training: 'This is my rifle [while slapping the rifle]; this is my gun [while slapping the genitals]; the one is for killing, the other for fun.' . . . I dreamed that even more boys and men will develop the affective, the tender and the relational in themselves, and abandon all urges towards heroics. . . . I dreamed of a long-lasting applause when we welcome Gorbachev in our countries, and of the beneficent, hope-giving trust we have in his actions. And finally, I dreamed of peace in the heart, a healing of all rifts and ruptures, of the *shalom* in which everything and everyone participates, and of the peace which the world cannot give but for which we must hold ourselves open. . . .

And I heard again the words of Psalm 8, as adapted by Diewerke Folkertsma, a mother receiving welfare: 'From our lofty positions, we have thrown away our dignity in defiance; from being landlords, we have become exploiters . . . Lord our God, teach us to discover that enough is Enough. . . .'

And now it is dark. I see the small sickle of a rising moon, and a few stars. And I think of 'all creation' . . . I wish that the cyclical thinking which has retained its place in the liturgy together with organic thinking would again be appreciated. Only in this way can the pressure to get ahead, to succeed, to be out in front, making history, be interrupted again and again. Then we can remain united with the whole of creation without women holding rituals, when the moon is full, in order to honour the goddess. That looks to me like a step backwards! . . .

In principle, we already live in the new creation, on the basis of the incarnation and the descent of the Spirit 'on all flesh'. She, the *ruach*, is the love-filled and communicative power exchanged between Jesus and his '*Abba*'. And 'Our Mother, the Holy Spirit', invites us to a life in relationships; relationships between people, nations, races and classes, both homosexual and heterosexual; and between people and animals, flowers, plants and things.

Just as woman is identified with Wisdom in the Hebrew Bible, so also is the Spirit the image of the all-analysing and intellectual knowledge, of the surpassing knowledge of the heart, of love. She is the 'light in the darkness and refreshment in the heat of the day'. To her we sing at Pentecost:

Purify what is blemished;
Give water to the withered;
Heal the wounded.
Make the rigid pliable,
Warm the chilled,
Lead back to true paths those who have wandered.

The *ruach*, the Spirit, gives us new life, and lets us breathe more freely, lets us catch our breath. But she is also the storm, the wind and the fire. . . .

Therefore we pray: 'Send forth your Spirit and all shall be recreated.' And the face of the earth will be renewed. . . .

Pentecost, 1989

BIBLIOGRAPHY

Achterberg, W., 'Op zoek naar een ecologische ethiek', in Achterberg, W., and Zweers, W., edd., *Milieucrisis en Filosofie* (Amsterdam: Van Arkel, 1984), pp. 142–71.

Achterhuis, H., 'De boom des levens: mythe of realiteit?', in Achterhuis, H., *Over bomen gesproken* (Baarn: Ambo, 1985), pp. 113–45.

Achterhuis, H., 'Het milieu als "commons"', in Achterberg, W., and Zweers, W., edd., *Milieufilosofie* (Utrecht: Van Arkel, 1986), pp. 201–31.

Bal, M., 'Sexuality, Sin, and Sorrow. The Emergence of the Female Character (A Reading of Genesis 1–3)', in *Poetics Today* 6.1–2 (1985), pp. 21–42.

Barbour, I. G., *Technology, Environment and Human Values* (New York, 1980).

Bateson, G., *Steps to an Ecology of Mind* (St Albans, 1973).

Beemer, T., 'De Schrift als bron van inzicht voor een christelijke sexuele moraal', in *Schrift* 112 (1987), pp. 131–5.

Bennema, P., 'Een spoor van de geheel Andere: Over de bedreigende en bevrijdende werking van natuurwetenschappen voor het geloof' in *Tijdschrift voor Geestelijk Leven* 42.4 (1986), pp. 403–21.

Bennema, P., and Hoefnagels, P., 'Thermodynamica, Milieu en Maatschappij', in *Sociologie als Engagement: In dialoog met Harry Hoefnagels* (Zeist: Kerkebosch, 1987).

Berman, M., *The Reenchantment of the World* (New York, 1984).

Bianchi, E. C., 'The Super-Bowl Culture of Male Violence', in Bianchi, E. C., and Ruether, R. R., edd., *From Machismo to Mutuality* (New York, 1976), pp. 54–70.

Bianchi, E. C., 'Psychic Celibacy and the Quest for Mutuality', in ibid., pp. 87–101.

Birch, C., 'Creation, Technology and Human Survival: Called to Replenish the Earth', in *The Ecumenical Review* (1976), pp. 66–79.

Bloch, M. and Bloch, J. H., 'Women and the Dialectics of Nature in Eighteenth-Century French Thought', in MacCormack, C. P., and Strathern, M., edd., *Nature, Culture and Gender* (New York/Melbourne, 1980), pp. 25–42.

Blommestijn, H., 'Menswording, een goddelijk geboorteproces: Irenaeüs van Lyon', in *Speling* 40.4 (1988), pp. 86–94.

Bookchin, M., *The Ecology of Freedom: The Emergence and Dissolution of Hierarchy* (Palo Alto, 1982).

Borremans, V., 'Conviviale technologie voor vrouwen', in *Streven*, January 1983, pp. 299–310.

Bouma, H., *Kunnen we maar niet beter zwijgen* (Kampen: Kok, 1988).

Bovenschen, S., *Die imaginierte Weiblichkeit* (Frankfurt, 1979).

Braidotti, R., 'De politiek van de ontologische differentie', in *Tijdschrift voor Vrouwenstudies* 36.4 (1988), pp. 375–90.

Brinkgreve, C., *De belasting van de bevrijding* (Nijmegen: SUN, 1988).

Brinkman, M. E., *Het leven als teken* (Baarn: Ten Have, 1986).

Brinkman, M. E., 'De ambivalentie van het begrip "behoud van de schepping"', in *Geest en Leven* 65.2 (1968), pp. 100–9.

Brinkman, M. E., 'De verwevenheid van schepping en sacrament: Neiuwe perspectieven vanuit de oecumenische discussie', in *Tijdschrift voor Theologie* 29.1 (1989), pp. 38–55.

Bulhof, I. N., 'Solidair met de natuur', in KTUU Addresses to Academic Sessions, 1989.

Bultmann, R., *Glauben en Verstehen I–IV* (Tubingen, 1933–65).

Callenbach, E., *Ectopia* (Berkeley, 1975).

Capra, F., *Uncommon Wisdom* (New York/London, 1988).

Carmody, J., *Ecology and Religion* (New York, 1983).

Carson, R., *Silent Spring* (London, 1963).

Case-Winters, A., *God's Power: Traditional Understandings and Contemporary Challenges* (Westminster/John Knox Press, 1990).

Chodorow, N. 'Family Structure and Feminine Personality', in Rosaldo, M. Z., and Lamphere, L., edd., *Woman, Culture and Society* (Stanford, 1974), pp. 43–67.

Chodorow, N., *The Reproduction of Mothering: Psycho-Analysis and the Sociology of Gender* (University of California Press, 1978).

Cobb, Jr., J. B., 'Feminism and Process Thought', in Greeve

Davey, S., ed., *Feminism and Process Thought* (New York/ Toronto, 1981), pp. 32–62.

Collier-Bendelow, M., *Gott ist unsere Mutter* (Freiburg, 1989).

Conciliar Proces, thematic issue of *Wending* 43.4 (1988).

Conciliar Proces (Het), thematic issue of *Speling* 40.4 (1988).

Couwenberg, S. W., 'Op zoek naar nieuwe spiritualiteit', in *Civis Mundi* 26.2 (1987), pp. 45–51.

Dawson Scanzoni, L., 'The Great Chain of Being and the Chain of Command', in Kalven, J., and Buckley, M. I., *Women's Spirit Bonding* (New York, 1984), pp. 41–56.

Deckers, W., *Het onzichtbare gelaat* (Berchem, 1986).

De Lange, H. M., *Wij moeten ons haasten* (Kampen: Kok, 1988).

Delhaye, K., 'Chercher la femme chez Foucault', in *Krisis* 30.1 (1988), pp. 57–64.

Dembowski, H., 'Ansatz und Umrisse einer Theologie der Natur', in *Evangelische Theologie* (1977), pp. 47ff.

Dessaur, C. I., *De achste scheppingsdag* (Arnhem: Gouda Quint, 1988).

Diekstra, R. W. F., *Hoe geestelijk is gezondheid?* (Deventer, Bohn, Staffleu en Van Loghum, 1988).

Dodson Gray, E., *Why the Green Nigger?* (Wellesley, 1979).

Dodson Gray, E., *Patriarchy as a Conceptual Trap* (Wellesley, 1982).

Dodson Gray, E., 'A Critique of Dominion Theology', in Hessel, D. T., ed., *For Creation's Sake* (Philadelphia, 1985), pp. 71–84.

Douglass, J. D., *Women, Freedom, and Calvin* (Westminster Press, 1985).

Duchrow, U., and Liedke, G., *Schalom* (Stuttgart, 1987).

Duintjer, O., *Hints voor een diagnose* (Baarn: Ambo, 1988).

Duquoc, C., 'Mensch/Ebenbild Gottes', in Eicher, P., ed., *Neues Handbuch theologischer Grundbegriffe*, vol. 3 (Munich, 1985), pp. 83–94.

Easlea, B., *Witch-Hunting, Magic and the New Philosophy* (Brighton, 1980).

Ecumenical Decade 1988–1998: Churches in Solidarity with Women, thematic issue of *Women in a Changing World* 23 (June 1987), World Council of Churches.

Episcopal Conference (Letter from the Netherlands), *Bondgeno ten in God's Schepping?* (Utrecht, 1989).

Fabella, M. M. V., and Oduyoye, M. A., *With Passion and Compassion* (Maryknoll, 1988).

Faricy, R. J., 'The Person-Nature Split: Ecology, Women, and Human Life', in *The Irish Theological Quarterly* 53.3 (1987), pp. 201–18.

Farrington, B., *The Philosophy of Francis Bacon* (Liverpool, 1964).

Fox Keller, E., 'Nature as "Her"', in *Proceedings at the Second Sex Conference*, September 1979.

Fox Keller, E., *Reflections on Gender and Science* (New Haven/London, 1985).

Fox Keller, E., and Grontkowski, C. R., 'The Mind's Eye', in Harding, S., ed., *Discovering Reality* (Dordrecht/Boston/London, 1983), pp. 207–24.

Friedan, B., *The Feminine Mystique* (London/New York, 1971).

Fromm, E., *To Have or to Be?* (London, 1978).

Fuchs, G., '"Öko statt Ego": New-Age-Spiritualität und christlicher Glaube', in *Diakonia* 18.4 (1987), pp. 254–60.

Ganoczy, A., *Der schöpferische Mensch und die Schöpfung Gottes* (Mainz, 1976).

Ganoczy, A., *Schöpfungslehre* (Düsseldorf, 1983).

Ganoczy, A., and Schmid, J., *Schöpfung und Kreativität* (Düsseldorf, 1981).

George, S., 'Interview by Henk Donkers and Paul Hoebink', in *N. C. R. Handelsblad*, 31 January 1989.

Gerstenberger, E. S., *Jahwe: Ein patriarchaler Gott?* (Stuttgart/Berlin, 1988).

Gilligan, C., *In a Different Voice* (Cambridge, Mass., 1982).

Gilligan, C., 'A Different Voice in Moral Decisions', in Eck, D. L., and Jain, D., edd., *Speaking of Faith* (London/New Delhi, 1986), pp. 221–30.

Göttner-Abendroth, H., *Das Matriarchat I* (Stuttgart/Berlin, 1988).

Gremmen, C. C. M., and Westerbeek van Eerten, J. A., *De kracht van macht* (Den Haag, 1988).

Grey, M., *Redeeming the Dream: Feminism, Redemption and Christian Tradition* (London/New York, 1989).

Grey, M., *Weaving New Connections: The Promise of Feminist Process Thought for Christian Theology* (Nijmegen, 1989).

Griffin, S., *Woman and Nature* (New York/Cambridge, 1978).

Griffin, S., *Pornography and Silence* (New York, 1981).

Grossmann, S., 'Schöpfer und Schöpfung in der feministischen Theologie', in Altner, G., *Ökologische Theologie* (Stuttgart, 1989), pp. 213–34.

Halkes, C. J. M., *Zoekend naar wat verloren ging* (Baarn: Ten Have, 1984).

Halkes, C. J. M., *Feminisme en spiritualiteit* (Baarn: Ten Have, 1986).

Halkes, C. J. M., and Van Heyst, A., 'Simonis en de "vrouwelijke" natuur', in *Mara* 1.1 (1987), pp. 5–15.

Häring, B., *Frei in Christus, Band 1* (Freiburg im Breisgau, 1979).

Hauke, M., *Die Problematik um das Frauenpriestertum vor dem Hintergrund der Schöpfungs und Erlösungsordnung* (Paderborn, 1982).

Hens-Piazza, G., 'A Theology of Ecology: God's Image and the Natural World', in *Biblical Theology Bulletin* 13.4 (1983), pp. 107–10.

Heyward, I. C., *The Redemption of God* (Washington, DC, 1982).

Heyward, I. C., *Our Passion for Justice* (New York, 1984).

Houtepen, A., *Theology of the 'Saeculum': A Study of the Concept of 'Saeculum' in the Documents of Vatican II and of the World Council of Churches, 1961–1972* (Kampen, n. d.).

Houtepen, A., 'Gerechtigheid, vrede en zorg voor al wat van God is', in *Geest en Leven* 65.2 (1988), pp. 109–18.

Houtepen, A., 'Oecumene in een fantastische cultuur', in *Kosmos en Oecumene* 22 (1908), pp. 7–8.

Huizer, G., 'The Anthropology of Crisis: Participatory Action Research and Healing Witchcraft', paper for the Bob Scholte Memorial Conference, Amsterdam, 14–16 December 1988, Third World Center, Nijmegen, pp. 1–44.

Imbens-Fransen, A., *Daar kun je maar beter (niet) over praten*, workbook on the problem of incest and religious education (Delft: Meinema, 1987).

The Integrity of Creation, thematic issue of *Women in a Changing World*, World Council of Churches, 26 (June 1988).

Introducing the Ecumenical Decade for Churches in Solidarity with Women, thematic issue of *The Ecumenical Review* 40.1 (1988).

John Paul II, Apostolic Letter *Mulieris Dignitatem*.

Johnson, E. A., 'The Incomprehensibility of God and the Image of God Male and Female', in *Theological Studies* 45 (1984), pp. 441–65.

Justice, Peace and the Integrity of Creation, thematic issue of *The Ecumenical Review* 38.3 (1986).

King, U., 'Women in Dialogue: A New Vision of Ecumenism', in *Heythrop Journal* 26 (1985), pp. 125–42.

King, U., *Women and Spirituality* (London, 1989).

King, Y., 'Making the World Live: Feminism and the Domination of Nature', in Kalven, J., and Buckley, M. I. edd., *Women's Spirit Bonding* (New York, 1984), pp. 56–67.

Korff, W., 'Frau/Man', in Eicher, P., ed., *Neues Handbuch theologischer Grundbegriffe*, vol. 1 (Munich, 1984), pp. 361–8.

Krattiger Tinga, U., 'Neue Worte, alte Tätze', in Schmidt-Biesalski, A., ed., *Befreit zu Rede und Tanz: Frauen umschreiben ihr Gottesbild* (Stuttgart, 1989).

Kuhn, T., *The Structure of Scientific Revolutions* (Chicago, 1962).

Kwee Swan-Liat, 'Wonen en werken op de kleine aarde', in Achterberg, W., and Zweers, W., edd., *Milieufilosofie* (Utrecht: Van Arkel, 1986), pp. 231–57.

Leland, S., 'Feminism and Ecology: Theoretical Connections', in Caldecott, L., and Leland, S., edd., *Reclaim the Earth* (London, 1983), pp. 67–73.

Lemaire, T., 'De Indiaanse houding tegenover de natuur', in Achterberg, W., and Zweers, W., edd., *Milieucrisis en Filosofie* (Amsterdam: Van Arkel, 1984), pp. 171–89.

Lemaire, T., 'Tussen wildernis en Arcadië', in Achterhuis, H., *Over bomen geproken* (Baarn: Ambo, 1985), pp. 11–45.

Lemaire, T., *De Indiaan in ons bewustzijn* (Baarn: Ambo, 1986).

Lemaire, T., 'Een nieuwe aarde (utopie en ecologie)', in Achterberg, W., and Zweers, W., edd., *Mielieufilosofie* (Utrecht: Van Arkel, 1986), pp. 257–89.

Lemaire, T., *Binnenwegen* (Baarn: Ambo, 1988).

Lerner, G., *The Creation of Patriarchy* (New York/London, 1986).

Liedke, G., *Im Bauch des Fisches* (Stuttgart, 1979).

Link, C., *Die Welt als Gleichnis* (Munich, 1976).

Link, C., 'Die Debatte über die Theologie de Natur', in *Spiritualteit en werken aan de toekomst*, Multidisciplinary Centre for Church and Society, Driebergen, contribution to the conciliar process (Driebergen-Rijsenburg, 1987).

Loades, A., ed., *Feminist Theology: A Reader* (Westminster/John Knox Press, 1990).

Loenen, D., *Sokrates in gesprek* (Amsterdam, 1966).

MacCormack, C. P., 'Nature, Culture, and Gender: A critique', in MacCormack, C. P., and Strathern, M., edd., *Nature, Culture and Gender* (New York/Melbourne, 1980), pp. 1–25.

Manenschijn, G., *Geplunderde aarde, getergde hemel* (Baarn: Ten Have, 1988).

McDaniel, J. B., *Of God and Pelicans: A Theology of Reverence for Life* (Westminster/John Knox Press, 1989).

McFague, S., *Metaphorical Theology* (London, 1983).

McFague, S., *Models of God* (London, 1987).

McMillan, C., *Women, Reason and Nature* (Oxford, 1982).

Merchant, C., *The Death of Nature* (San Francisco, 1980).

Meyer-Abich, K. M., 'Zum Begriff einer praktischen Theologie der Natur', in *Evangelische Theologie* (1977), pp. 3ff.

Meyer-Wilmes-Müller, H., 'Menschenbild und sexualität', in Kassel, M., *Feministische Theologie* (Stuttgart, 1988), pp. 105–37.

Mies, M., *Patriarchy and Accumulation on a World Scale* (New Jersey/London: Zed Books, 1986).

Mohn, G., *Frieden in der Schöpfung* (Gütersloh, 1987).

Mol, A., '"Sekse" en "wetenschap": een vergelijking met twee onbekenden', in De Vries, G., ed., *Wetenschapstheorie: De empirische wending* (Groningen Wolters-Noordhoff, 1989), pp. 97–107.

Moller Okin, S., *Women in Western Political Thought* (Princeton, NJ, 1979).

Moltmann, J., *Trinität und Reich Gottes* (Munich, 1980) – ET, *The Trinity and the Kingdom of God* (London: SCM, 1981).

Moltmann, J., *Gott in der Schöpfung* (Munich, 1985) – ET, *God in Creation* (London: SCM, 1985).

Moltmann, J., 'Heeft de moderne samenleving een toekomst?', lecture delivered in University of Groningen, 26 May 1988.

Moltmann-Wendel, E., ed., *Weiblichkeit in der Theologie: Verdrängung und Wiederkehr* (Gütersloh, 1988).

Mulack, C., *Im Anfang war die Wahrheit* (Stuttgart, 1988).

Mulder, E., *Freud en Orpheus* (Utrecht: Hes, 1987).

Nature, thematic issue of *Women of Power* 9 (1988).

Nelson, J. B., *Embodiment* (Minneapolis, 1978).

Nelson, J. B., *The Intimate Connection* (Philadelphia, 1988; London, 1992).

Ortner, S., 'Is Female to Male as Nature is to Culture?', in Rosaldo, M. Z., and Lamphere, L., edd., *Women, Culture and Society* (Stanford, 1974).

Outshoorn, J., *Een irriterend onderwerp* (Nijmegen: SUN, 1989).

Parvey, C. F., *The Community of Women and Men in the Church*, The Sheffield Report (Geneva, 1983).

Pastoral Constitution on the Church in the Modern World (Gaudium et Spes) (London: Catholic Truth Society; n.d.).

Pohier, J., 'The Power of Blessing over Psychic Identity: an interview with Françoise Dolto', in *Concilium* 2 (1985), pp. 70–83.

Raiser, K., 'Wie weit trägt die ökumenische Utopie?', in *Evangelische Kummentare*, June 1988.

Rang, B., '"Geleerde vrouwen van alle Eeuwen ende Volkeren, zelfs by de barbarische Scythen." De catalogi van geleerden vrouwen in de zeventiende en achttiende eeuw', in *Geleerde vrouwen, Jaarboek voor Vrouwengeschiedenis*, vol. 9 (Nijmegen: SUN, 1988), pp. 36–65.

Rang, B., 'Wat heeft het Cartesiaanse denken vrouwen opeleverd?' in *K. U. Nieuws* 18 (1989), pp. 10–11.

Ransijn, P., 'Opkomst van een nieuw religieus paradigma', in *Civis Mundi* 26.2 (1987), pp. 85–8.

Rhodes, L. N., *Co-Creating: A Feminist Vision of Ministry* (Westminster Press, 1987).

Ridderbos, S. J., *Eros bij Plato* (Kampen: Kok, 1988).

Rietdijk, C. W., 'De moderne fysica: suggestie van een verborgen werkelijkheid', in *Civis Mundi* 26.2 (1987), pp. 74–81.

Risseeuw, C., *The Fish Don't Talk About the Water* (New York/Leiden, 1988).

Robinson, J. A. T., *Truth is Two-Eyed* (London: SCM, 1979).

Röper, A., *Ist Gott ein Mann? Ein Gespräch mit Karl Rahner* (Dusseldorf, 1979).

Rosaldo, M. Z., 'Woman, Culture, and Society: A Theoretical Overview', in Rosaldo, M. Z., and Lamphere, L., edd., *Woman, Culture and Society* (Stanford, 1974).

Rosaldo, M. Z., 'Gebruik en misbruik van de antropologie', in *Jaarboek voor Vrouwengeschiedenis*, vol. 3 (Nijmegen: SUN, 1980), pp. 171–207.

Ross, S., 'Vrouwenlichamen en sacramenten', in *De Bazuin* 72.14, 7 April 1989, pp. 8–9.

Ross, S., 'Het lichaam als beeld van God', in *De Bazuin* 72.15, 14 April 1989, pp. 8–11.

Roszak, T., *Making of a Counter-Counter: Reflections on the Technocratic Society and its Useful Opposition* (New York/ London 1970).

Rubin, G., 'The Traffic in Women: Notes on the "Political Economy" of Sex', in Reiter, R. R., ed., *Towards an Anthropology of Women* (New York/London, 1975), pp. 157–211.

Rübsamen, R., 'Patriarchat: der (un)-heimliche Inhalt der Naturwissenschaft und Technique', in Pusch, L. F., *Feminismus-Inspektion der Herrenkultur: Ein Handbuch* (Frankfurt a. M., 1983), pp. 290–307.

Ruether, R. R., 'Sexism and the Liberation of Women', in Bianchi, E. C., and Ruether, R. R., edd., *From Machismo to Mutuality* (New York, 1976), pp. 70–87.

Ruether, R. R., *Sexism and God-Talk: Toward a Feminist Theology* (Boston, 1983), pp. 214–34.

Russell, L. M., *Human Liberation in a Feminist Perspective – A Theology* (Westminster Press, 1974).

Russell, L. M., *Household of Freedom: Authority in Feminist Theology* (Westminster Press, 1987).

Russell, L. M., ed., *The Liberating Word: A Guide to Non-Sexist Interpretation of the Bible* (Westminster Press, 1976).

Russell, L. M., ed., *Feminist Interpretation of the Bible* (Westminster Press, 1985).

Russell, L. M., et al., edd., *Inheriting Our Mothers' Gardens: Feminist Theology in Third World Perspective* (Westminster Press, 1988).

Schillebeeckx, E., *Gerechtigkeit en Liefde* (Bloemendaal, 1989).

Schmidt-Biesalski, A., ed., *Befreit zu Rede und Tanz: Frauen umschreiben ihr Gottesbild* (Stuttgart, 1989).

Schottroff, L., 'Gods verbond met Noah: Bibelstudie over Genesis 8.20–9.17', in Sölle, D., and Schottroff, L., edd., *Mijn broeders hoedster* (Baarn: Ten Have, 1986), pp. 17–33.

Schroevers, P., 'Inhoud en betekenis van een holistisch natuur-beeld', in Achterberg, W., and Zweers, W., edd., *Milieucrisis en Filosofie* (Amsterdam: Van Arkel, 1984), pp. 49–74.

Schumacher, E. F., *Small is Beautiful* (London, 1973).

Schumacher, E. F., *A Guide for the Perplexed* (London, 1977).

Schwarzer, A., 'Interview door Malou van Hintum', in *K. U. Nieuws* 22 (1989), pp. 10–11.

Science and Technology, thematic issue of *Women of Power* 11 (1988).

Smith, J. M., ed., *Women, Faith, and Economic Justice* (Westminster Press, 1985).

Smuts, J. C., *Holism and Evolution* (London, 1926).

Soelle, D., *The Strength of the Weak: Toward a Christian Feminist Identity* (Westminster Press, 1984).

Sölle, D., *God heeft mensen nodig* (Baarn: Ten Have, 1984).

Spretnak, C., *The Politics of Women's Spirituality* (New York, 1982).

Spretnak, C., and Capra, F., *Green Politics* (London: Paladin, 1985).

Studium Generale, *Documentatie: Veranderend Natuurbegrip* (K. U. Nijmegen, 1989).

Stufkens, H., *Gezichten van de nieuwe tijd* (Amstelveen, Luyten, 1984).

Stufkens, H., *Heimwee naar God* (Rotterdam: Lemniscaat, 1987).

Swidler, L., *Biblical Affirmations of Woman* (Westminster Press, 1979).

Tavard, G. H., *Woman in Christian Tradition* (Notre Dame, 1973).

Van den Berg, J. H., *Metabletica* (Nijkerk: Callenbach, 1957).

Van Dijk, P., *Anders over de 'schepping' denken*, pp. 173–88.

Van Dijk-Hemmes, F., 'Bijbellezen "als een vrouw"', in *Schrift* 122 (1989), pp. 43–9.

Van Dijk-Hemmes, F., 'Herschappen tot een levende tora: Het verbond bij Hosea, Jesaja en Jeremia', in *Sleutelen aan het verbond* (Boxtel: Katholieke Bijbelstichting, 1989), pp. 52–75.

Van Dongen, M., 'Tegenstelling in eenheid: Erotiek en mystiek in het werk van Etty Hillesum', in *Lust en Gratie* 22, pp. 8–24.

Van Gennep, F. O., *Mensen hebben mensen nodig* (Baarn: Ten Have, 1972).

Van Leeuwen, A. T., *Christianity in World History* (London, 1964).

Van Steenbergen, B., 'Spiritualiteit in de Nieuwe Tijd', in *Civis Mundi* 26.2 (1987), pp. 51–7.

Van Wolde, E. J., 'Genieten van liefde en lijden onder

verlies: Hooglied en Genesis 2–3', in *Schrift* 110 (1987), pp. 78–86.

Van Wolde, E. J., *A Semiotic Analysis of Genesis 2–3* (Assen, 1989).

Van Zoest, P., 'Theologie en New Age-holisme', in *Civis Mundi* 26.2 (1987), pp. 57–60.

Verbond voor het leven, (Een), Dutch Council of Churches, Amersfoort, Horstink, no date.

Verdegaal, K., 'De mens als beeld van God', in *Shrift* 87 (1983), pp. 87–93.

Vink, C., 'New Age en Rationaliteit', in *Civis Mundi* 26 (1987), pp. 60–7.

Von Rad, G., 'Das theologische Problem des alttestamentlichen Schöpfungsglaubens', in *Gesammelte Studien* (München, 1958).

Van Rad, G., *Weisheit in Isräel* (Neukirchen, 1970) – ET, *Wisdom in Israel* (London: SCM, 1972).

Van Weizsäcker, C. F., *De tijd dringt* (Baarn: Ten Have, 1987).

Von Werlhof, C., Mies, M., and Bennholdt-Thomse, V., *Frauen, die letzte Kolonie* (Reinbek bei Hamburg, 1983/1988).

Walton, J., 'Ecclesiastical and Feminist Blessing: Women as Objects and Subjects of the Power of Blessing', in *Concilium* 2 (1985), pp. 63–70.

Webster, J. C. B., and Low, E., edd., *The Church and Women in the Third World* (Westminster Press, 1985).

Westermann, C., *Der Segen in der Bibel und im Handeln der Kirche* (München, 1968).

Westermann, C., *Erträge der Forschung: Genesis 1–11* (Darmstadt, 1972).

Wildiers, M., *Theologie op nieuwe wegen* (Kampen: Kok, 1985).

Winnicot, D. W., *Playing and Reality* (New York, 1971).

Wiskerke, N., 'New Age-Holisme en Scheppingstheologie: Visies op mens en natuur', in Chowdhury, T., et al., *Holisme en New Age-bewustzijn* (Tilburg, 1986), pp. 139–204.

Wiskerke, N., *Meeleven met de schepping* (Delft: Meinema, 1988).

Wolthuis, M., *Alles uit één*, doctoral thesis, University of Nijmegen, 1986.

Women, Science, and Society, thematic issue of *Signs* 4.1 (1978).

Women: Sex and Sexuality, thematic issue of *Signs* 5.4 (1980).

Women and Violence, thematic issue of *Signs* 8.3 (1983).

Women's Experience and the Sacred, thematic issue of *Women of Power* 12 (1989).

'Workshop on Integrity of Creation, "Experiencing Oneness: Caring for All"', in *Towards an Ecumenical Theology of Creation* (Geneva: World Council of Churches, 1987), pp. 1–5.

Zweers, W., 'Milieufilosofie: Een inleidende oriëntatie', in Achterberg, W., and Zweers, W., edd., *Milieucrisis en Filosofie* (Amsterdam: Van Arkel, 1984), pp. 7–24.

Zweers, W., 'Natuur en cultuur en ecologisch perspectief', in Achterberg, W., and Zweers, W., edd., *Milieucrisis en Filosofie* (Amsterdam: Van Arkel, 1984), pp. 97–142.

Zweers, W., 'Varianten van ecologische ervaring', in Achterberg, W., and Zweers, W., edd., *Milieufilosofie* (Utrecht: Van Arkel, 1986), pp. 19–73.

INDEX

Achterberg, W. 80
Achterhuis, H. 118–19
Aeschylus 43
Agricola 21
Albert the Great 59
Améry, C. 80
Andrea, J. V. 25, 30
Antonelli, J. 121
Aristotle 3, 4, 34, 41–4, 59, 65
Athanasius 132

Bacon, F. 4, 19, 27–31, 33, 35,
  49–50, 56–9, 77, 104, 168
Barbour, I. G. 86
Barth, K. 79
Bateson, G. 99
Beemer, T. 135
Bennema, P. 8, 99
Berman, M. 98
Bernard of Clairvaux 157
Bianchi, E. C. 144–5, 149
Bloch, J. 64–5, 67–8, 70
Bloch, M. 64–5, 67–8, 70
Blommestijn, H. 131
Bookchin, M. 111
Borremans, V. 159–60
Bovenschen, S. 69–73
Brinkman, M. E. 78, 90
Bultmann, R. 78–9

Callenbach, E. 111
Campanella, T. 25–30
Capra, F. 74, 96, 98–9, 113–15,
  120, 123, 125–6
Carson, R. 108
Chodorow, N. 13, 14
Copernicus 78
Couwenberg, S. W. 122
Cox, H. 119

de Beauvoir, S. 12
Descartes, R. 31, 33, 35–6, 40, 77,
  79, 95–6, 118
Diekstra, R. W. F. 100
Donne, J. 21
Drewermann, E. 80
Duintjer, O. 38
Duquoc, C. 130–1, 133

Empedocles 34
Engels, F. 112

Farrington, B. 27–30, 57
Flaubert, G. 72–3
Folkertsma, D. 161
Fox Keller, E. 7, 50–4, 56, 57–8,
  60, 62, 92, 100–7
Freud, S. 69
Freidan, B. 108–9
Fromm, E. 113

Galileo 78
Ganoczy, A. 89
George, S. 159
Gilligan, C. 14
Glanvil, J. 60
Goethe, J. W. 72
Goodfield, J. 104
Göttner-Abendroth, H. 112
Gray, D. 149
Greefkens, I. 147
Gregory of Nyssa 76, 131, 132
Grey, M. 150
Griffin, S. 146–7

Halkes, C. J. M. 66, 142
Hall, F. 46–7
Häring, B. 136, 140
Hauke, M. 139

Hermes Trismegistos 58
Holm, L. 48
Horowitz, M. 43
Houtepen, A. 89, 119
Hugh of St Victor 76–7
Huizer, G. 8, 105

Ibsen, H. 149
Irenaeus 131–2

Janeway, E. 70
John of Salisbury 24
John Paul II, Pope 134
Johnson, L. B. 144

Kant, I. 40
Kelly, P. 115
Kent Rush, A. 125
King, Y. 112–13
Korff, W. 135
Kuhn, T. S. 51, 96
Kwee Swan-Liat 95

Lamartine, A. 115
Lawrence, D. H. 146–7
Leland, S. 112
Lemaire, T. 48–9, 80, 90, 111–12
Lerner, G. 41–4
Levinas, E. 118
Levi-Strauss, C. 17
Liedke, G. 7, 34, 39, 45, 76, 77,
    78–80, 82–3, 90, 92
Lucretius 34

MacCormack, C. 10, 16–17
Marcuse, H. 111
McClintock, B. 105–6
McFague, S. 152–3
Merchant, C. 7, 20–4, 26, 28–32,
    45, 60, 69, 110
Mies, M. 46–7
Miller, H. 146
Milton, J. 21
Moller Okin, S. 44, 68
Moltmann, J. 78, 83, 84–8, 91,
    120, 122, 125, 127

Nelson, J. B. 144–6

Newton, I. 91, 96
Nicholas of Cusa 24
Nixon, R. M. 144

Ortega y Gasset, J. 49
Ortner, S. B. 9–16, 68
Outshoorn, J. 50

Painter, T. S. 104
Paracelsus 59–60
Patton, G. 144
Paul, St 138, 141
Picht, G. 34
Plato 4, 50–1, 53, 57
Pliny 21
Polanyi, M. 104

Rahner, K. 140
Ransijn, P. 124
Reddock, R. 46
Reeves Sanday, P. 145
Reitdijk, C. W. 97
Risseeuw, C. 47, 105
Robinson, J. A. T. 123
Roosevelt, T. 144
Roper, A. 140
Rosaldo, M. Z. 16–17
Roszak, T. 124
Rousseau, J. J. 63–70
Rubin, G. 50
Ruether, R. 109, 111, 150

Sartre, J.-P. 118–19
Scheffler, M. 70–2
Scheler, M. 70–1
Schillebeeckx, E. 136
Schroevers, P. 92–3
Schumacher, E. G. 95–6
Schwarzer, A. 146, 148
Simmel, G. 101
Simonis, A. J. 6, 137–9, 141
Simonton, O. K. 99
Smit, J. 115
Smuts, J. C. 123
Solle, D. 91
Spinoza 91
Spretnak, C. 113–15, 120–1, 123,
    125

Starhawk 125
Strathern, M. 10
Stufkens, H. 123

Tavard, G. 128, 131, 139
Temple, W. 91
Tennyson, A. 49

Van den Berg, J. H. 48
Van Dijk, P. 91
Van Gennep, F. O. 134
Van Leeuwen, A. T. 118–19
Van Steenbergen, B. 90, 96, 97, 124

Van Wolde, E. 134
Vaughan, T. 60
Von Rad, G. 79, 83
Von Weizacker, C. F. 39

Weber, M. 90
Westermann, C. 81–2
White, L. 80
Whitehead, A. N. 97
Winnicot, D. W. 102
Wiskerke, N. 86, 125, 127
Wolthuis, M. 123

Zweers, W. 93–4